UNDER THE HAT

UNDER

MEMOIR OF AN
UNSTOPPABLE
WOMAN TRAILBLAZER

THE HAT

FLORENCE KLEIN

Published by Prestige Words
Bainbridge Island, Washington

Cover and interior book design by Mi Ae Lipe (whatnowdesign.com).
Front and back cover photos by Jerry Davis.
Printed in the United States of America.

To contact the author or order additional copies:
FlorenceUnderTheHat@gmail.com
FlorenceUnderTheHat.com

First Edition, April 2023
Print book ISBN: 979-8-218-13482-2
Ebook ISBN: 979-8-218-13483-9
Library of Congress Control Number: 2023900648

To my children —

Karen Andre

Kim Susan

Jeffrey Samuel

— who have never stopped loving their trailblazing mother

CONTENTS

INTRODUCTION

There is a type of woman who cannot remain at home.
In spite of the place her children and family fill in her life,
her nature demands something more—she cannot divorce herself
from the larger social life. She cannot let her children narrow her horizons.
For such a woman, there is no rest.

— Golda Meir —

These were the words I carried in my wallet for many years.

They, along with an early epiphany I had when I was twelve, have inspired me to help family, friends, colleagues, acquaintances, and strangers alike weather countless challenges, changes, and circumstances in their lives, just as they did in mine.

My name is Florence Klein. I'm more than eighty years old, and I'm a trailblazer.

I say that not with ego, but simply because it is true. I was likely the first female stockbroker in Philadelphia, the first woman real estate developer to convert old factory buildings into residences, and someone whose idea of giving back to the community was to visit prisoners in one of the most maximum-security facilities on earth because no one else would.

And that's just the beginning of a lifetime of crazy adventures.

I honestly had no idea that I was a trailblazer until I turned eighty-two and others began pointing out how remarkable my life has been. Until then, I had never stopped to reflect on who I was—I simply went out and *did*. And I had a blast doing it.

What can I say now to invite you into my life? A life that I never could have imagined, a life that I'm still blessed beyond measure to be continuing with excitement, joy, and wonder.

I'm a woman who is always looking forward to the future, indeed—one who has always pursued her inner drive and sense of responsibility to make a difference. And I still feel compelled to offer help and guidance to younger generations in their own pursuit of courage, purpose, and compassion. This book is the result. As my son Jeff has said, "Mom, each chapter could be a book!"

Join me and travel with me.

Florence Klein
March 2023, Bainbridge Island, Washington

Remember always that you have not only the right to be an individual—
you have an obligation to be one.

— Eleanor Roosevelt —

1
A PHILADELPHIA CHILDHOOD

Father ~ On the Move ~ A Shocking Early Lesson ~
Settling Down, Finally ~ Family Memories ~
Grandma Ida ~ An Epiphany ~ Mother

I have to be in charge of my life.
— Florence Klein —

My father Joseph was born in Poland in 1908 and immigrated to the United States in 1921 when he was thirteen, coming through Ellis Island in New York along with his mother Sarah, two older brothers, and four sisters. In fact, the entire extended Rosenthal family emigrated from Poland to Philadelphia at around the same time. They were all master tailors, and his brothers Abe and Sam would ultimately establish their own shops in north Philadelphia, where they were respected for their craftsmanship by their retail customers.

My father reached working age at a difficult time. When the United States stock market crashed in the fall of 1929, it triggered the Great Depression and the worst financial recession in modern history, which would last about a decade. By the time my parents married in 1932, finances were already tight. My father worked primarily for wholesale clothing manufacturers of women's suits and coats, where he was paid a fixed rate for each item he completed. I can still see him sitting at the kitchen table counting his tickets for the garments he finished that week. The work was seasonal, but for many weeks there was simply none to be had because the demand for consumer goods had fallen so precipitously during the Depression.

My parents started out living in the Germantown area of Philadelphia, where I was born at the nearby Temple Hospital in 1934. Less than a year later, we moved to the Logan neighborhood in north Philadelphia (4900 Franklin Street) for a short time. But year-round work was still impossible to find in Philly, so we moved from Philadelphia to Brooklyn in 1936 when I was around two years old—in hopes of finding steadier work. My brother Lewis was born in 1938 in Brooklyn.

When we lived in New York, I remember how I loved walking around Coney Island, with my brunette curls bouncing, wearing a beautiful light blue coat that

Me with my parents at Coney Island.

Father had made me. He used a sewing machine to complete a garment, but he always made hems and linings by hand. I could never see these stitches because they were so small and fine. (In fact, he was still making beautifully tailored suits for me when I became a stockbroker in 1965. Amazingly, almost five decades later, I wore one of these handsome suits to a Rotary Club meeting this year—and it still fits!) He also made an exquisite pin with my initials "FR" (Florence Rosenthal), which I still treasure and enjoy wearing on jackets.

My father was a warm, quiet person who smiled easily. He never spoke ill about or demeaned anyone. I admired his conscientiousness about work and his concern for punctuality. He did not drink, smoke, or crack jokes, nor was he interested in sports, but he did like playing pinochle and the card game Casino. He also enjoyed *The Forward*, a widely read Jewish newspaper that was published in Yiddish until English was added in the 1980s. Like most people at that time, he spent many hours listening to the news on the radio about World War II.

I also learned the meaning of honesty from him. He was very fair and honest with his customers and never lied to anyone. I was very young when Father would give me a quarter to go down to the grocer on the corner to buy a loaf of bread, which cost only twenty-two cents at that time. It never occurred to me to buy a stick of licorice for myself, which I loved (and still do), and not return the two or three cents of change. I still remember how responsible I felt in carrying out this important task.

ON THE MOVE

With reliable work still in short supply, even in New York, my father moved us back to Philadelphia in 1938. After yet another scarce season, my parents tried running a small retail dress shop on Seventh Street in South Philly. Customers still didn't have the money to buy dresses, so my parents were forced to close this store. My father then returned to working at a garment factory, possibly Redman Brothers. We moved back to Logan to 5900 Hutchinson Street when I was five, this time to a big house with very steep front steps across the street from the Birney Elementary School playground. I loved living near the school and sitting on our enclosed front porch watching other little girls playing jump rope during recess, especially when I was confined after getting chicken pox. I also met my first real friend who was my own age there, Hilda.

So, I was sad when we moved again in 1940, this time to 8515 Germantown Avenue, where Father opened his first tailoring shop. We lived upstairs from the business on this very busy avenue, which is the longest continuous street with street-cars in Philly (about six miles). Germantown has always been a heavily commercial area, even during Revolutionary War times, and it is home to nearly thirty historical landmarks. It was also where the first-ever American protest against slavery was held and where one of the few remaining houses on the Underground Railroad still exists.

It was here where I started school at the Jenks Story Jenks Elementary (as it was called back then), which was only 125 child-size steps from my house. My first experiences were delightful ones—I remember being happy just skipping down the sidewalk to go to school. In fact, soon after I started kindergarten, I got let out to recess one day and then ran home, thinking I'd just say hello to my brother and Mother. This was an early start in exploring and trying out new ideas on my own!

Within a year or two, when I was in second grade, Father found yet another storefront space with living quarters at-tached, this time at 3002 Wharton Street in southwest Philly in an area known as

Me at around two years old.

Grays Ferry. Since Wharton was another busy commercial street, he felt it was a good location to start a more ambitious tailoring business. Now that the end of World War II was approaching and bringing with it some prosperity to local neighborhoods, Father was feeling more optimistic about brighter times ahead, and he was overjoyed to open this new store that bore his own name—Rosenthal's Tai-loring. Later, he added a clothes-cleaning operation to his business. While Mother waited on customers at the front of the store, he worked in the back. I can still hear the slamming thud of his large pressing machine as it landed hard down on the clothes that he had repaired or ones his customers brought in to have "only pressed."

Top: Row houses in north Philadelphia, like the kind I grew up with. Above: This image from Google Street View, photographed in October 2019, shows homes directly across from my father's store and our home on 3002 Wharton Street. (The building was torn down and is an empty lot.) Here, you can see the open porches I remember so well, which provided both an outdoor sitting area and significant extra storage space.

By this time, my father established his store in the front part of our house on the first floor, while our living, dining, and kitchen areas lay directly behind it. Behind the kitchen door was a small, paved yard with a high wooden fence; here my brother and I could safely play without my mother worrying about us. I liked being in our closed backyard behind the store, where I could jump rope and stay in charge of my younger brother, who was always pleasant. Steep, curved stairs led upstairs to our three bedrooms.

This house was in a white, mostly Catholic, working-class neighborhood with typical Philadelphia row houses with porches that abutted the sidewalk on the north side of the street. Meanwhile, our small business and home stood on the south side—one of the many that were owned and operated by Jewish families. Soon I was enrolled in a new school, Acorn Elementary. But this time, Father had to walk me to school since it was four and a half blocks away.

A Shocking Early Lesson

Soon after we moved into our new home, racism invaded my innocence one sunny fall day as I was skipping home from school with my Black classmate Agnes. Happily giggling as eight-year-old girls do when their arms are linked together, I suddenly became aware of people staring at us. There sat several middle-aged white women on open front porches looking at us, aghast.

As I glanced up at them, I remember feeling a bit puzzled at first that they were looking at me. Why? They had never spoken to or paid any attention to me, even though I lived right across the street from them. But there was no mistaking their disapproval in their hard gaze at us.

Nonetheless, Agnes did not say anything or indicate that she had noticed their stares. We continued skipping down the block on the north side of Wharton Street, our contrastingly colored arms still linked together. As those Catholic women watched us, they said not a word. They didn't have to. I instinctively felt their silence—and knew what it meant. How dare I, a little Jewish girl, stride down their side of the street—let alone arm in arm with a colored girl!

Even now, this incident stands out vividly in my mind, an unerasable, indelible moment. I can still feel the chill of their cold looks from their open front porches as if it happened yesterday. And in that instant, I learned about racial discrimination.

I must say that, being Jewish, I did not know much about the Catholic religion at that time. However, since I was curious, I went with one of my classmates on a Saturday to her neighborhood church, where I saw her go into a booth for confession. She explained that confession was where you could tell your sins to a priest so that God could forgive you.

What sins could an eight-year-old possibly have to confess? I thought.

Settling Down, Finally

By 1944, World War II was still being fought but money was steadily coming in for us, finally. With finances stable for the first time in their lives, my parents could buy a row home of their own with an open front porch—and so we moved back to the Logan neighborhood to live at 4819 North Eighth Street. At last, after moving eight times by the time I turned ten, we'd found the home we'd stay in for the rest of my childhood.

And now I was back at Birney Elementary, but this time, instead of living right across from the school and wistfully only getting to watch other children attend it, I was walking four blocks myself as a fifth grader. I was so excited!

Our newfound stability meant that I could not only start but actually keep new friendships. On Saturday afternoons my mother, Lew, and I would go down to my father's store. Dad would go earlier in the day, and I would visit my friend Ruth one block east on Wharton Street. Her parents also had a small retail business at the front of their living quarters. I would sit on their soft, brown sofa listening to her take piano lessons from a tall, rather wide, authoritative teacher. I had thoughts that I might like to play the piano myself, but it was not a burning desire, nor did I have a piano at home or would ever even dream to ask my parents for such an expensive item. Ruth and I deeply enjoyed our friendship and, as we got older, we invited other girls and then boys to join us for "socials." Ultimately, I'd ask Ruth to be my maid of honor at my wedding in 1954.

One of the best parts about moving back to our "new" old neighborhood was that I was now old enough to rediscover and explore it on my own. Soon I began figuring out new routes to walk home. In the process, I discovered streets previously unbeknownst to me that were full of those famous Philadelphia row houses, as well as a few hazards along the way. One day, as I returned from the library, I ended up getting thwarted by train tracks, so I had to backtrack the entire way I'd come. Another time I almost smashed my hand trying to playfully fling myself over the metal railings on the stairs leading up to the front of these row houses. It was a good thing that my overprotective mother never knew of these little adventures!

Family Memories

In the 1940s, everyone was concerned about World War II, and we were no exception. We studiously collected cans and bottles, aware of our government's directions to Americans to save money and buy bonds to help fund US involvement in the war. As an eleven-year-old in 1945, I wanted to do my little part toward the war effort too. I'd earmark two dollars a week from my seventy-five-cent-an-hour babysitting job and hand this cash to a teacher, who collected money from students in my class and made sure the funds were properly donated. Hundreds of

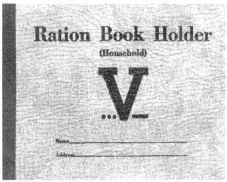

Left: A WWII poster advertising the school collection of money for the war effort. Above: My family's ration book. These wartime holders contained stamps for rationed items like sugar, meat, cooking oil, and canned goods. A person could not buy a rationed item without presenting the requisite stamp.

thousands of schools across America participated simultaneously in this "Schools at War" program from 1942 to 1945, raising more than two billion dollars toward the war effort—the equivalent of nearly thirty-one billion dollars in today's money.

Thus, my introduction to fiscal responsibility started early, and it didn't stop there. Once a week, I'd walk the five blocks from our house to the (PSFS) Philadelphia Savings and Loan Association on Broad Street, and a teller would take my little bank book, mark the amount of cash I was depositing into my account, and then make the deposit. (A bank book was a small physical book given to a new account holder, similar to a modern-day check register. Although in this era of debit cards and electronic payments, does anyone even remember check registers anymore?)

Not everything in my childhood was serious. We had moments of family fun, with warm memories of going to Willow Grove Park, an amusement park about twenty-five minutes from our home by trolley. I would go on the Thunderbolt roller-coaster with my brother; sometimes my father would join us, but my mother would not. I enjoyed the Ferris wheel, the merry-go-round, the cotton candy, and the booths where one could pitch balls to earn a prize. Occasionally, we'd take an open-air trolley through the Fairmount Park forest to Woodside Park, another Philadelphia amusement park that was just as delightful. Sadly, Woodside closed in 1955 and Willow Grove followed in 1975—the latter turned into a shopping mall. It was another sign of the changing times.

At home, we lived a simple life with few routines. My mother was not particularly talented in the kitchen and preferred making simple meals. Following the Jewish tradition, my mother, as the woman of the house, would light two candles to greet Shabbat (the Sabbath), which begins at sundown on Friday night and ends on Saturday sundown. (Incidentally, Sabbath candlesticks make a lovely wedding gift for a new Jewish couple. I inherited my grandmother Ida's beautiful brass ones many decades ago and still feel blessed to light them each Friday evening to this day.)

We observed all the major Jewish holidays, including Rosh Hashanah (the New Year) and Yom Kippur, the holiest day of the year with its solemn religious fast. For a short time in fifth or sixth grade, I attended Sunday school. My brother also had a bar mitzvah, the coming-of-age rite at thirteen (although I did not have a bat mitzvah, the equivalent for girls, because it wasn't as common at that time).

I enjoyed going with my mother, father, and brother Lewis on Sundays to visit my paternal grandmother, Sarah. We didn't own an automobile, so we'd take public trolleys and subways instead. Sometimes we stopped on South Street at our favorite delicatessen on the way. How I loved the corned beef or beef tongue sandwich on Jewish rye with a sour pickle and a sour tomato; Lew liked the corned beef special with Russian dressing. (I believe Philadelphia has the best delis outside of New York City to this day!)

I still remember a wonderful candy store with a soda fountain that sat on the corner on the same side of the street as our house. They had double-dip banana splits with sprinkles and chocolate syrup, but my favorite was the black-and-white ice cream sodas (today they're just called chocolate and vanilla—but they're still just as delicious). I'd usually take my ice cream home, but it sure was a treat to sit on the stool at that soda fountain.

My brother Lew and I rarely fought. I was four years older, but we always felt close to each other. He was a cute little boy with a big smile and a twinkle in his beautiful blue eyes. Like my son Jeff, he made friends very easily. He was slim, ran track in high school, and was always fond of sports. He was also an avid collector of baseball cards and at one time had a very extensive collection. It's been more than ten years since he's been gone, and I deeply miss him.

Reading and history were my favorite subjects in school. I was a good student, but I do not recall having any favorite teachers. I also didn't mind school's rules or repetition; what I did love best about it was learning new ideas and about the world.

I don't remember ever playing with dolls or having a favorite blanket or toy. Really, my favorite pastime was simply reading. My favorite books included *Rumpelstiltskin*, *Little Women*, and *Mary Poppins*. I loved walking the ten or twelve blocks by myself to and from the Logan Library, and my mother could not understand why I brought so many books home. This large, local library was part of a system founded by Benjamin Franklin— yes, that Ben Franklin. When I was ten years old or so, I was always sneaking peeks in the adult section, although I wasn't interested in the love stories—I was simply curious to see subjects different from

My brother Lew and I.

what was in the juvenile genre. Like countless children all over America, I'd hide books under my blanket at bedtime and read them with a flashlight so Mother would not see me.

When I was ten or eleven, I'd buy movie magazines at the local store—they cost fifteen cents a copy—and read them on our front porch. I also collected pictures of movie stars like Bette Davis, Cary Grant, Rita Hayworth, and Merle Oberon (many people, even recently, have mentioned that I look like her).

As I mentioned before, both of my parents—as Americans—listened intently to the radio during the war and especially to President Franklin Delano Roosevelt's famous Fireside Chats for the latest news of the Nazi invasion and other developments; these radio addresses were calming and inspirational. I can still see my father crouched down to tune in.

I, on the other hand, listened to radio stories and soon became addicted. I loved walking the four blocks home from Birney Elementary every weekday at noon for lunch, past the row houses and their open porches. While I ate, Mother and I would listen to the popular daytime radio shows of the day: the soap opera *Our Gal Sunday*, the daytime drama *When a Girl Marries*, and the soap opera *One*

Man's Family. Usually, at the end of lunch, we listened to Kate Smith, an American contralto who was known as the First Lady of Radio. She was famous for opening the New York Yankees games with her rendition of "God Bless America."

In the evening, I'd be captivated by such legendary serial adventure stories as *The Green Hornet, Captain Midnight* (yes, I sent away for the magic ring), and *The Shadow Knows* ("Who knows what evil lurks in the hearts of men? The Shadow knows!").

Other entertainers we enjoyed during the war years and in the 1950s were Bing Crosby with his very popular song "White Christmas," as well as Bob Hope, an actor and a comedian known for his one-liners and for entertaining the WWII servicemen overseas. We also loved Liberace. In his later life, he became famous for his flamboyant performances and lifestyle, but he originally began as a child prodigy who sang and played the piano, especially the boogie blues; he was very popular when I was growing up.

We didn't get a television in our home until I was about twelve or thirteen, but sometimes I'd go to someone else's home to watch a program on their small televisions. We did have a telephone in our house, but it was a black stationary phone with dials—no cell phones in those days! We had what was called a "party line"; three or four other homes would all be connected through the same circuit. If you raised the receiver, you might hear another "party" on the line, and you'd have to hang up the phone and try again later. You didn't use the phone for long conversations, and the only choice you had was AT&T!

GRANDMA IDA

When I was quite young, my Grandma Ida rode the bus about an hour from her home in Trenton, New Jersey, about thirty-five miles from Philadelphia. She'd come to see us at least every six weeks. She did not really like my father, but she never said anything rude about him or argued with him. I really looked forward to her visits and so did my mother, and Ida eagerly anticipated seeing us as well.

But what I really loved was going by myself to visit her. My mother and I would walk the two blocks to Roosevelt Boulevard and wait on the south side of this well-known, tree-lined, multilane highway at the corner of Ninth Street for the green-and-white bus to pick me up. Carrying my little suitcase and eager to board, I'd usually sit in one of the front seats. (I still sit in front seats on buses if they're available.) Naturally, I was absolutely entranced by this forty-minute trip—looking out the windows, I was curious about everything I saw along the way.

When I got to my stop, I'd hop out, and Grandma Ida would always be waiting for me at the bottom of the hill. I was never concerned that she wouldn't. She did not hug or kiss me, but she was always certainly pleased to see me. We then walked up the hill on Market Street (at that time it seemed quite steep to a small child), and our next stop was always at the bakery to pick up our challah bread, since it was usually a Friday, and the Jewish weekly tradition was to have challah for the Sabbath. Because her oven wasn't functioning at home, Grandma had dropped off the dough on her way down the hill to pick me up, and the bakery would bake it for her.

Wherever we went, Ida Richmond was always greeted with respect. I felt it and knew it, even at my young age. I would hear the merchants' admiration as they spoke with her, in the way they talked politely and deferentially. A small, thin woman, she looked like the classic grandmother with white hair in a bun atop her head. She always carried herself with dignity, and everyone around her responded to her calm presence accordingly.

After picking up our freshly baked, warm challah, we'd continue up the hill for about three blocks to 242 Jackson Street, a home she had been living in for many years. There I'd see her father, my great-grandfather, Lewis Albert. I can still picture him sitting on the low side of the two wooden steps outside of the house. The warmth and sweetness of this man with his long white beard have resonated inside of me these many, many years. He loved that I wore white gloves with my best dresses! My son Jeffrey has the same lovely demeanor and sweet quality as this great-great-grandfather of his.

A rare photo of me at around age seven with Grandma Ida and brother Lew at age four.

Ida Richmond was a slight woman who came over from Poland with her two brothers Louis and Jacob and two sisters in 1885. She was in the Spanish-American War somehow, but exactly in what capacity was unknown to my family; she never spoke about it at all. She would have been eighteen at the time. Perhaps she was a nurse, but it seems unlikely as she was not a caregiver type. She could have been a spy, some sort of gopher, a fundraiser for the war effort, or a documenter. This war lasted only four months, and I am still trying to find out why she received a rather substantial monthly pension, which I only discovered when I found a notice from the Veterans Administration in her belongings.

Ida married in 1905 when she was twenty-six, which was considered rather old in those times for a young girl to stay single. In this way, she was very much like her daughter, my mother.

As was often the case in that era, Grandma never spoke about her background. She was stoic and forthright—you always knew where she stood on any person or issue. In fact, she was much like my daughter Karen is today. Grandma was very opinionated and made no secret of the fact that she liked only honest, truthful, and intelligent people. If she saw someone coming down her side of the street whom she did not care for, she quickly crossed the street so as not to have to interact with them. And she'd rarely if ever say why she did not want to meet whoever was walking toward us. Occasionally, she might concede, "Oh, that person is not a good person" or "He was not reliable."

And she held grudges. If she thought a sister or a friend had misled her, she refused to speak to them for months. In fact, one of her sisters lived on the same side of Jackson Street just a few houses away. But Grandma did not care for her sisters and rarely spoke fondly of them. In fact, I cannot even recall any dinners where we went to my aunts' homes.

Grandma Ida's two-story house was small, with an alley on one side that led into a large (or what appeared to be large to me) yard that was planted with some tall trees, several rosebushes, and other flowers. Grandma was not a gardener, but she did know the names of her trees. I loved to play in her pretty yard by myself and dream up different names and games.

Her house was clean, not messy, and it had a beautiful wooden rocking chair that I have in my living room now. I also remember a large wood-and-glass cabinet about five feet tall that contained beautiful glasses and lovely bowls. I always admired this cabinet of hers, and years later when I found a similar one in an antique sale, I purchased it—it still reminds me of Grandma Ida. When I stayed with her, I'd sleep on a high green daybed by the front window of the house. But memory (or a lack thereof) is a funny thing; to this day, I simply cannot remember where she slept.

Every Christmas, Easter, and summer when there was no school, I would be at 242 Jackson Street. No dolls or toys did Grandma Ida have, but I'd go upstairs to the floor above to play games with her neighbor's two daughters. Grandma never did any of the usual stereotypical "grandmotherly" things: she didn't read to me or tell me stories, nor did she seem to have much of a sense of humor.

Like my mother, she was not interested in cooking. Her son Emil would always bemoan her horrible, boring meals. Grandma Ida was, however, very strict about the Jewish rules for keeping kosher as well as observing the Sabbath, which meant that she did not cook from Friday night to Saturday night. As is the Jewish religious custom, she'd make some sort of a stew on Friday afternoon and maintain a low fire on the stove to keep it heated, as any sort of food preparation was considered work that was forbidden on the Sabbath. Her stew often contained meat with carrots and celery, and perhaps we'd have a baked potato. Sometimes there was chicken or just a watery chicken soup, while cornflakes and milk were usually available for breakfast.

From her, I noticed how she carried herself as a businessperson and how deeply she was respected for her knowledge and experience. Her innate strength and conviction served as a strong female role model for me. She was industrious, intelligent, assertive, and always calm and serious; I never once saw her yell, scream, throw anything, or cause a scene. Most of all, I witnessed and felt her quiet, supreme independence.

Strict, observant Orthodox Jews do not work, ride, shop, carry money, or cook from after Friday sundown until Saturday sundown. That limited what we could do on Saturdays, but it was the day we could visit her "rich" brother in his home on Richey Place, which we'd do once or twice a month when I was staying with her. We'd arise early and depart when Grandma was ready to start out, her handkerchief wrapped around her door key.

Her brother lived about four miles away, and we walked—or rather, Grandma sprinted while I with my short legs rushed, trotted, or ran to keep up with her. Then she, never raising her voice or saying anything, would wait at the intersections for me. As fast as she walked, her piercing blue eyes never missed an object lying on the pavement. I'd be walking (mostly behind her) and see her bend down and then turn toward me with a one-dollar bill or a silver bracelet. I still have the bracelet!

Once we arrived at her brother's house, I was quite happy to see the beautiful double-seat swing where I could lift my tired feet off the ground. This was in a large, manicured garden that surrounded a very lovely, well-appointed home. I do remember how spacious it felt and how much I liked being in its rooms. We'd stay for a few hours.

Uncle I. H. (everyone called him that, not Louis) had a large rubber mill-machinery business called L. Albert & Son. He was also a Dollar-a-Year Man; that was an honor bestowed on designated executives and patriots who worked in companies that manufactured government defense supplies and necessary equipment during WWII; they were so named because they were paid only a dollar a year by the government for furthering the war effort. I liked Uncle I. H., but I rarely spoke to him (at that time children often didn't talk to grown-ups they weren't close to as much as they might today). His manner was friendly and warm, and I also liked his wife, who was polite, mannered, and pleasant.

After our visit, Grandma Ida and I would walk back home, a bit more slowly this time, unless we left after sundown, in which case Uncle I. H. would have us driven by car. Ida would always hurry through the cobblestone streets, turning the corners cautiously and rarely speaking a word. She was always sure of the next block, never doubting where the brick pavement dipped or had a crack. Her watchful steel-blue eyes saw everything and everyone coming toward us.

The late September air often held a slight chill that made me shudder, but I would speak not a word in complaint. It was Rosh Hashanah, the eve of the Jewish New Year, and we were moving quickly so as not to be late to the Great Synagogue.

Entering through its front doors, we'd immediately scamper up the stairs to the women's area. (Only men would be permitted to sit on the first floor, as this was an Orthodox *shul*, or synagogue, where men and women were not permitted to sit together.) Glancing quickly, Grandma would spot two seats in the middle of the fourth row on the balcony level—she always wanted to be in the center of a row in the many times I went with her. *Quiet!! Shhh! Shhh!* No sound dare I make as we settled into our seats without a hello or even an acknowledgment by any of the other women. This was clearly not a social event.

It was odd—everyone knew Grandma and yet I can hardly remember anyone speaking to Ida Richmond. And it seemed that those two seats for her and me were always empty in the middle of that balcony row. Once we sat down, I'd sit on the edge of my chair with my eyes glued to the floor below where the rabbi, or sometimes more than one, huddled on the *bimah*, a raised platform from where verses in Hebrew were chanted for this very special holiday. Grandma would follow the liturgy and the chanting and praying. The entire synagogue was lit by candles and a few enormous, splendid chandeliers—a beautiful sight that always inspired awe and reverent respect.

With my Shirley Temple curls and wearing my best dress and polished patent leather shoes, I found it very comfortable to be with my grandmother during these special times. The service would last about three or four hours, and once it was over, without stopping to speak to anyone, we'd move with the crowd and hurry back home to Jackson Street.

Once I became a teenager, I stopped spending these holidays with her, but I did go to see her often, and she attended my wedding in June 1954. When she grew older and could no longer see well, she'd walk with a baby carriage in front of her so no one would know that her vision was impaired. She continued to live alone in her home until she passed away in her nineties. Such a very proud and private individual.

An Epiphany

One day when I was twelve years old, I was struck by a personal revelation. I was standing in my bedroom by a wall on my left, facing my bed with the window on the opposite wall, when I said to myself, "*I HAVE TO BE IN CHARGE OF MY LIFE.*"

I instinctively knew right then and there that it was a singular statement and a very profound one for a twelve-year-old to declare in 1946. I cannot recall exactly what brought that thought forward, nor had I always held that statement in my conscious mind. But I do know that those words were destined to become a guiding force throughout my life. No one else was going to help me, nor could I rely on anyone but myself, so at that moment, I realized that this would have to be the way.

Mother

Perhaps I had this epiphany because I innately understood my mother. She was beautiful, kind, and good-hearted, but she was scared, overwrought with challenges, and unsure of herself. She also suffered from colitis, and for years she went regularly to a Dr. Zamostein, who lived around the corner on Louden Street. He recommended that she see a psychiatrist. As a teenager, I'd go with her, first on the trackless trolley, then on the Broad Street subway, and then on another trolley to West Philadelphia. The whole trip took about an hour each way. I'd sit in the outer office while she was with the doctor, and she never told me what he said or what she felt, but she always seemed a bit relieved as we were going back home. We went every two months for more than a year.

Her fears overruled her, but she never spoke about them, as was the custom in those times. Her physician's official diagnosis was neurotic depression and "hysterical personality"—in keeping with the common male-practitioner lingo at the time for many mental health issues among women—but there was little insight in those days as to the exact cause of her illness. Throughout my forties, I recall her undergoing several electroconvulsive treatments at Friends Hospital, a Philadelphia psychiatric hospital, where she'd stay one or two nights.

This was the common custom in those days, when sending electrical shocks to the brain was considered an effective intervention for treating severe depression, various forms of mania, and catatonia. Treatment and attitudes were so different back then before the advent of modern neuroscience. Nevertheless, she would improve for a time after her visits and be somewhat less anxious.

While I was still living at home, my sweet father would occasionally go around the corner to play pinochle with a few of the neighbor men, maybe once a month or so. But, within an hour, Mother would send me out to find him, saying she was sick and wanted him to come home. Father just accepted her condition and never raised his voice much.

My mother, Ruth Rebecca Albert Rosenthal (pictured on the next page as a child with her mother), had lived a difficult childhood that conditioned her adult life. Her own mother, the very stoic Ida Richmond (my beloved Grandma Ida), had married a very handsome man from a prosperous Trenton family. However, he was not a good husband; he left her on many occasions, was usually away from home, came back who knows how many times, fathered my mother, and fourteen years later fathered Emil, my mother's brother. My mother Ruth essentially raised Emil,

My parents with Lew at his bar mitzvah in 1953.

My grandmother Ida as a young mother, with her daughter Ruth, my mother.

and her relationship with him was overly protective and quite unusual. She never spoke about her father, and I never saw him either.

She never graduated from high school, and she married my father Joseph Rosenthal in her later twenties (considered an advanced age for those times). She did some clerical work for the Curtis Publishing Company when she was perhaps in her late fifties or sixties.

My mother was a kind, pleasant person who rarely raised her voice. Despite her mental and physical suffering, she was not demonstrative or negative, and her mood was never ugly. But she seldom expressed emotion and never cuddled or hugged me. Still, I knew she loved me, and I never felt neglected.

She never seemed to have any friends, either. I was surprised to discover from my own childhood playmates that they had mothers who were different from mine, cooking special meals for their families and socializing with female friends. I cannot recall anyone ever stopping by our house to gossip, talk, or do anything with my mother.

Indeed, she spoke only about her sisters-in-law, who were both named Anna. Anna Sam had one son, Jerry, who had worked as a technician at Einstein Medical Center in Philly and died in his forties, while Anna Abe had three sons, two of whom were physicians and the other an engineer. My mother really did not like the Annas, declaring that they were too demanding. Perhaps it was because my mother was so weak, and she felt inadequate next to them, but I never really knew why, and we never discussed the matter.

How sad, when I think of Mother now, and how alone she must have always felt. Even though she was extremely introverted, Mother did work in my father's business. As I recall, she seemed to have no problems meeting and talking with customers who came to the front of his store while he tailored and pressed clothes in the back. In fact, she seemed to quite enjoy it.

True to her quiet nature, my mother was quite overprotective about me and my brother Lewis, just as she had been with her own brother Emil. Among her many fears was infantile paralysis, or polio, which was indeed an extremely serious childhood illness before vaccines were invented. This cruel disease paralyzed many kids and debilitated them for life. In fact, I never learned to swim as a child because Mother never allowed my brother and me to take lessons; polio was commonly thought to be transmissible in swimming pools at the time.

Once, when I was gifted a pair of roller skates in the fifth or sixth grade, I had to plead mightily to be allowed to even put them on. Even then, I skated only on the street in front of our house while my mother dutifully watched from the open front porch. She also never allowed me to ride a bike.

With my beloved Uncle Emil when I was about three years old.

My father never said anything about her overprotectiveness, nor did he ever really complain about her. My parents rarely told me what to do or not do, and my mother never even looked at my homework or made any remarks if I didn't get good grades (which was quite unlike my high expectations with my own three children). But I never wished that they would have set more boundaries, expectations, or restrictions for me. Instead, I always felt happily independent, which I believe encouraged my natural curiosity, my keen appetite for exploration, and my pioneering spirit in my life and career. I also never felt neglected or unloved; I knew my parents loved me. And I had other supportive family members—my uncle Emil thought I was special, and Grandma Ida and I were unusually close.

Looking back, I have no doubt that my mother's greatest joys were me and my brother. Later it was her grandchildren, whom she absolutely adored. She was a fantastic knitter who made magnificent cross-stitch and embroidered tablecloths for me when I was married. And the sweaters she knitted for my children have remained in the family and now their own children wear them.

But Mother would sometimes warn me, "Don't think too much of yourself." Years later, when I visited a Jungian psychiatrist, I told him that I always wore hats. He said the hats related to my mother telling me to put a lid on my accomplishments, goals, and ideas. She always said I was "clearing on," a Yiddish expression meaning "always thinking." She never understood me, but that didn't make me feel bad or sad or angry—I truly felt self-sufficient, just a very happy little girl with a friendly smile who liked to read.

Even today, I look back on my childhood as being very pleasant. I was never bullied or made fun of in class or at home. And I was truly lucky—I must have had a sixth sense that I was—and would turn out to be—just fine.

2
ADOLESCENT FUN

**A Popular Girl ~ Adventures in Atlantic City ~
First Jobs ~ Attempts at Athletics, Typing, and College ~
Mother's Liberation**

And now that you don't have to be perfect, you can be good.
— *John Steinbeck,* East of Eden —

hysically, I developed early while we were living on North Eighth Street in Logan. It felt like all the boys from the neighborhood, high school, and even college liked me, and one of them was always wanting to walk me home.

For instance, there was Seymour Katz from the candy store on Seventh and Rockland Streets. He took a liking to me when I was in sixth or seventh grade (he was a little older than I), and he started hanging out in front of my house. I thought he was a little swarthy-looking, but it was nice that he came around. Later, he got in trouble in school and was suspended.

The boys thought I was very pretty and well-built. In fact, I was voted the girl with the best figure in ninth grade in a popularity contest when I graduated from junior high school. It made me feel good but not conceited. My mother always warned me, "Don't have a big head," so those words stayed in the back of my mind where they belonged.

Even though I got more dates than the other girls, that didn't make me gloss over or feel superior to them. Although I tried to get my best friends Ruth and Cyn dates, I wasn't that successful. I'd meet them in town at the large department stores like Strawbridge & Clothier or John Wanamaker to shop and have lunch. I remember trying my first Chinese food at the Cathay Tea Garden on Chestnut Street, and how happy I was to find a peach dress for eighteen dollars to wear to my graduation from Cooke Junior High.

Walking to school with other girls in Logan, I felt I was always on the edge of being "in the clique." Sometimes I was included and at other times not, but I always felt comfortable around these girls. But even in junior high school, I was never a gossiper and preferred to stick to serious subjects. I also always worked every Wednesday after school and all day on Saturdays. And I enjoyed it—my parents did not encourage or discourage me from working. These traits set me apart from my female peers, and I was fine with that.

My high school sorority dance in 1950, when I was president of Tau Epsilon Chi. I'm in the first row, third from the left.

I did have wonderful times dating as a teenager, but I just never fell head over heels with any of the boys. I enjoyed all the invitations to dances, socials, and fraternity parties at the University of Pennsylvania and clubs and sports at Drexel University. I was even named queen of the Valentine Dance and others—too long ago to remember them all.

My parents had no idea that on a few Saturday nights in high school, I'd have three dates for one evening. First up was going out for an afternoon walk with one boy; then I'd get dressed for a fraternity party with my number-two date. Finally,

I'd come home and get picked up around midnight to go sledding at the nearby public Ashbourne Country Club. What fun!

ADVENTURES IN ATLANTIC CITY

In my teenage years, my parents, Lew, and I would visit the beaches of Atlantic City, New Jersey, which was an hour-and-a-half ride from Philly. This was our annual family vacation, and even my mother enjoyed its famous Boardwalk and beach. It was great fun for Lew and me to rise at about eight in the morning, rent bicycles, and ride the five miles of the Boardwalk, which was the first and longest one in the country, having opened on June 26, 1870.

A crowd standing on the Atlantic City Boardwalk in front of the Blenheim Hotel in 1911.

In the 1940s, the Boardwalk was lined with many elegant hotels, such as the Traymore and the Claridge. We couldn't afford to stay at or dine in these places, but occasionally we'd wander into their grand, beautiful lobbies to look around. Sadly, the majestic Traymore was demolished in 1972 for financial reasons—not anticipating that the state would pass legalized gambling in 1976.

We usually rented a small apartment and stayed about two weeks. On Labor Day weekend, of course, there was always the very popular and exciting Miss America Pageant. I loved watching the glamorous contestants being driven in the

flashy convertibles along the Boardwalk. They'd be wearing their states' sashes over their bathing suits or, in some years, elegant gowns. We'd stand or if we were lucky, we'd get a rolling chair against the boardwalk rails and cheer as the young, gorgeous contestants floated by, waving. The boardwalk would be packed, and everyone enjoyed the long parade, the girls, and the entire event.

This annual pageant originally started in 1921 as a "bathing beauty revue" to showcase mostly physical beauty, figures, and smiles, with each contestant representing her specific state. Later, a talent component was added and more recently, interview questions. But the Miss America organization has been wracked by numerous scandals and accusations over the decades. Starting in 2019, the swimsuit competition was eliminated, and current contestants are no longer judged so much on physical appearance

Top: The Traymore Hotel and the Atlantic City Boardwalk depicted on a postcard, circa 1916. Above: Lew and I enjoying the beach in front of the Traymore.

Contestants line up in swimsuits at the Miss America pageant,
September 1953, at Convention Hall in Atlantic City.

as their poise, values, life aspirations, academic performance, and intelligence. But in spite of all the controversy and ensuing changes, it recently celebrated its centennial birthday, and the Pageant is still a major competition for young women between the ages of seventeen and twenty-five. Unfortunately, it is no longer held in Atlantic City.

Even though the original Miss America contestants were judged largely on their beauty, I truly enjoyed watching them in Atlantic City and for many years afterward on television, and I never felt it was demeaning to women. In the 1950s and '60s, I did not know about any of the ugliness or scandals. In fact, I myself competed in several small beauty contests, and while it was nice when I was chosen and crowned Miss Whatever, I never took the whole thing too seriously. It was just a fun event!

It was well before the #MeToo movement of 2017 when substantial allegations of widespread sexual misconduct hit the mainstream press, which revealed how so many Hollywood and media men were accused of more than casual inappropriate behavior toward women—as well as how long this had been going on. It certainly opened our eyes to how poorly females had been treated and how often they'd been taken advantage of by employers in their efforts to achieve career positions and contracts.

FIRST JOBS

During eighth grade when I was fourteen, a school notice went out for any student who might be interested in working a few hours a week. Several of us went down to Center City in Philadelphia, which meant taking the Broad Street subway to the Teachers' Credit Union. After being given some basic tests, I and three others had jobs!

Because of child protection laws, we were considered too young to work more than four hours a week. In fact, I was the only student who continually worked on Wednesday afternoons, performing basic filing and clerical operations. Ironically, many years later, after I became a professional stockbroker at Robinson & Co. and was looking for clients, the Teachers' Credit Union became one of my clients. I still have my original TCU ID card from my junior high school days!

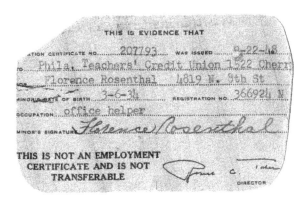

My identification card from the Teachers' Credit Union, where I got my first-ever job at age fourteen.

Another one of my first jobs was at Blauner's, a small department store in Philadelphia at Ninth and Market Streets, across from the Earle Theatre where Frank Sinatra and many other famous stars performed. (Not that I went to listen to him—I did not have that kind of money.) Once I turned sixteen, I could work longer hours. At Blauner's, I sold hats, which were located in the first aisle right near the front of the store. This was my introduction to wearing hats, and they've been my trademark all my life.

Later I worked at the much larger, higher-quality Strawbridge & Clothiers department store. This time I was stationed in the shoe department on the basement floor. It was tiring work, especially at Easter time, when I'd wait on customers, find shoes in the stacks, try them on the women and men, and attempt to convince them to make the purchase. I earned a commission on each shoe sale in addition to a wage of seventy-five cents an hour. I babysat too—also for seventy-five cents an hour back then.

Despite where I worked, I wasn't too tempted to spend my money. I'd buy a dress or sweater only occasionally for a date. I did love shoes, but even then, I'd rarely spend my small salary on any. By the time I reached high school, I was self-sufficient and never asked my parents for money.

ATTEMPTS AT ATHLETICS, TYPING, AND COLLEGE

Olney was a large high school with about 750 students when I attended from 1949 to 1952. To get to it, I had to take a bus from my home in Logan and then another one from 6460 North Sixteenth Street. (Yes, we had moved again!)

As a freshman, I decided to try out for the track team. It certainly seems odd now to think of me running track. I do not know why I thought I might like to run, but I can remember standing in the schoolyard where the girls lined up. I remember being dressed in a one-piece blue suit and the teacher in her gray gym clothes telling me, "Run a short distance as hard as you can and then make another try." Of course, I did not make the team—but I always viewed that attempt as a pleasant experience, not a defeat. I had never done any running and even by the age of sixteen, I'd never participated in any athletic sport (I was just too busy working).

But my favorite uncle, Emil, was a runner and my son Jeffrey is a runner and a head track coach, so the genes came through! I didn't learn to ride a bicycle until one of the boys helped me—maybe when I was fifteen—and I had to not let my nervous mother know about it.

I got through high school without much studying but lots of dating with many boys. I was known as "the cold fish" because I didn't "put out," drink, or smoke. I simply wasn't interested in sex, and fortunately, no one tried to force themselves on me. Back then, there was more decorum, formality, and restraint than today. I was also influenced by learning about syphilis in school and how serious STDs could be. And I had no desire to try any drugs. (My classmates and I knew at the time that marijuana existed, but I don't recall ever seeing it or being offered it in high school.)

The Remington Rand Model 85 bookkeeping machine, circa 1944 to 1950.

Between working and dating, I did somehow find time to take five academic courses in high school, thanks to studies in English, algebra, French, history, and bookkeeping and stenography (I do not believe the latter is taught anymore). I flunked French 4 and Health 3, but otherwise, I was an average student. I didn't feel any academic pressure from my parents, teachers, or anyone, for that matter.

In one of my first jobs, I learned to use a Remington Rand Model 85 bookkeeping machine, which was basically a manual typewriter topped with an awkwardly massive, top-heavy attachment that functioned as a bookkeeping machine. The entire beast was all metal—not a single plastic part at that time—and, along with its own custom stand, probably weighed close to a couple of hundred pounds. The keyboard consisted of a row of ten tabulator keys at the front, followed by a row of digit keys behind it, a space bar, and then three rows of a QWERTY typewriter keyboard. Most of all, I remember its wide carriage with a toothed metal bar and fourteen sliding mechanisms, which you could physically push from one side to the other with a most satisfying thunk. This was cutting-edge technology for the 1940s, and it made an impression (literally)!

In eleventh grade, I applied for a secretarial job at a clothing manufacturing plant on Twelfth Street in Center City. After having taken classes in stenography, dictation, typing, and accounting, I landed this position. But it was probably the worst job I ever had! Miss Rosenberg was my supervisor, a small, olive-skinned woman with a large beak nose and beady black eyes. We used typewriters to fill out forms that came in multiple tear-off sheets known as carbon copies. (Does anyone reading this even know what those are anymore?) I can still hear Miss Rosenberg's voice urging me to hurry as she hovered over me while my fingers fumbled to open those onionskin-thin carbon pages. I always needed two copies because I'd mess up. Then I'd still have to try to fix my mistakes using white correction fluid to get those papers perfect. I did not last long!

I had always wanted to go to college. Within weeks of graduating from high school, I left for Pennsylvania State University. How happy and excited I was to be living on the beautiful, expansive main campus in the municipality of State College, Pennsylvania. How I loved my psychology, art history, and philosophy courses, as well as my initial major in hotel administration. I even became a finalist in the Miss Independent Penn State competition, which honored physical beauty and academic performance.

So, I felt quite sad when I had to leave the school after two years because I could not afford the $275 for the spring term of 1953. But later I was able to

My mother in my kitchen in Dresher, Pennsylvania, around 1979. By this time, after suffering from decades of severe anxiety, she had finally found some happiness and peace in her later life.

obtain my full bachelor's degree in business administration from the Wharton School of the University of Pennsylvania in 1979 while I was working as a registered financial representative at Bache Halsey Stuart Shields.

MOTHER'S LIBERATION

When I was in high school, my mother didn't pay much attention to me—she couldn't really, with her condition. She continued to experience fainting spells. Years later, even when I was a married woman working full-time for a Philadelphia brokerage firm, I'd get calls from her at six in the morning while I was dressing and trying to get three young children off to school. Mother, in the throes of a full-blown panic attack, would declare over the phone, "Florence, I'm fainting—help me!"

I handled it by speaking softly, never yelling but firmly saying, "Mother, just lie down and you will feel better. Take a glass of water and get some fresh air." I remember those calls happening multiple times a week and can still hear the plaintive urgency in her voice and feel the awfulness of not being able to help her.

Many years later, after she died at the age of seventy-seven, I gave this eulogy at her funeral on January 24, 1983:

> *She was humble, but not shy. She was forthright and independent. She displayed and left us with strength as she went through her struggles through her many illnesses, always with a determination to survive and live. We were so happy that in these last years, I felt somehow my mother became liberated.*

Indeed, in her later life, my mother finally experienced a degree of freedom and relief. After Father died, she moved to an apartment across from my brother and sister-in-law Sharon. There at long last, she found friendship with a contemporary—a lovely woman who lived in the next block with whom she spent considerable time walking and talking together.

Mother also derived tremendous pleasure and joy in spending time with her grandchildren. Meeting one of the Kennedys—yes, of *that* Kennedy family—by chance at the airport was also deeply exciting for her.

Finally making these human connections was a way forward from her anxiety. And such deep anxiety she had suffered over much of her life, along with her colitis and all! Undoubtedly it manifested in her extreme overprotectiveness of Lew, in how she would phone me in the early mornings to help with her panic attacks, and in her calling for Father to come home from his beloved pinochle games with the neighborhood men. That anxiety was a deeply intrinsic part of her being, and to be freed from the worst of it brought happiness to those of us who loved her.

3
A FAMILY OF MY OWN

Len Klein ~ Early Married Life ~
Working Woman ~ Marie ~ Family Fun ~
Karen Andre ~ Kim Susan ~ Jeffrey Samuel ~ Marital Drifting

Integrity and truthfulness are the foundations upon which I raised my children.
— Florence Klein —

On June 13, 1954, I married Len Klein. It was a gorgeous, picture-perfect summer day, and I was just twenty years old. Our beautiful wedding took place outdoors in a very lush setting at the Curtis Arboretum in Wyncote, Pennsylvania. About 110 guests attended, including my brother Lew, mother Ruth, father Joseph, and grandmothers Sarah and Ida. On the groom's side was Len's mother Reba, father Sam, brothers Sid and Stanley, and daughter-in-law Myrna, plus many aunts, uncles, cousins, and friends from both sides of our families.

But the day before, I realized that I should not be getting married. I was simply too young. However, it was too late to cancel the wedding—that would hurt and distress my mother terribly, so I married a very nice, handsome, warm Jewish boy who I knew loved me very much.

Although the Korean War had officially ended in July 1953, the United States government was still drafting young men into the military, and so Len left Philadelphia in the fall after we were married. After completing basic training, he was stationed in the military town of Newport News, Virginia, with the US Army's Transportation Corp, which shipped missiles to various bases to support the overseas troops. Within six months, I followed him to our first home in Newport News. When I stepped off the Amtrak train at the Richmond station, I was shocked to find restrooms with large signs with arrows over the doors: **White | Colored**. I had never been in the South before.

EARLY MARRIED LIFE
In the early years of our married life in Virginia, I got a job as a cost accountant for Hampton Homes, a nearby construction company. Adele, my associate in our small

Getting ready on my wedding day on June 13, 1954.

office, dumbfounded me one day when she asked, "Do Jewish people really have tails? And horns behind their ears? I've heard about it." Just how do you answer that? Having spent most of my life in Philadelphia, home to a large Jewish population, I could not believe that she had never met any Jewish people. And how could she possibly not know anything about the Second World War or the Holocaust?

Len and I loved being close to Williamsburg and exploring its history and beaches, making new friends, and enjoying the weather. Even though I had never been in a drama club or done any acting in high school, I tried out for and received the lead in a play called *Night of January 16th*, put on by a local theater. This experience of being in my first play was so much fun, and my character's name was Karen Andre. I liked it so much that I later named my first child after it.

Len and I did not ever discuss not having children—it was just assumed in those years that one would have them after marriage. I originally thought I'd like to

My mother Ruth and Len's mother Reba on my wedding day to Len.

have five. After I started working in 1963 and had a miscarriage, I was very pleased and relieved to ultimately give birth to three normal, healthy children. I never ever thought it was a chore to have a family. Even in today's tumultuous world, I'd still decide to have children. The joy, love, pride, and growth that I have experienced in them are incalculable.

Len and I soon purchased a home on Fairfax Avenue in Newport News, and Karen was born in 1957. Len's father, a very warm, friendly man, died in 1958, a day after Karen's first birthday. Soon after that, Len's older brother Sid asked him to be a partner in Klein's Market, a third-generation grocery store in north Philadelphia. It was a difficult decision for Len, as he had other aspirations in the transportation field and never was too keen on the store. He was now a civilian

Above: On my wedding day on June 13, 1954. From left to right: My brother Lew, my grandmothers Ida and Sarah, my father Joseph, my mother Ruth, me, Len, Len's mother Reba, Len's father Sam, Len's brothers Sid and sister-in-law Myrna, and brother Stanley. Below: Len and me as we crossed a threshold.

Our honeymoon sendoff the day after our wedding.

working for the Army, but eventually he decided to help continue his family's business. Soon we moved back up north to our hometown of Philly.

WORKING WOMAN

By the time I turned twenty-nine, we had three small children aged two, four, and six, as well as a lovely split-level home in the northern Philadelphia suburb of Dresher. But I knew that I could not be satisfied, since working from home was not an option in 1963. Since junior high school, I had always enjoyed working, earning

Five generations of Kleins in their family grocery store in Philadelphia.

my own funds, and feeling independent. I found that doing what was expected of a suburban housewife and homemaker in those days, such as "play school" (holding small children's parties with the neighbors' or friends' children for an hour or two), hosting tea parties, and being a volunteer teacher's assistant was boring and intellectually unchallenging.

I soon found employment as a cost accountant in the aircraft financing department of the Denson Company, about a ten-minute drive from my home in an industrial park. But after a year and a half, the work became monotonous and the opportunities for advancement were limited. I needed something more stimulating. Really, perhaps the most fun I had on the job was flying with the owner to see one of his clients.

So, I began looking for a different career. I researched different newly emerging businesses that might offer stimulating careers and economic advancement, but the possibilities were far more limited for women than men. After making some inquiries and perusing the *Wall Street Journal*, I noticed that the field of hospital administration seemed to be growing. I was considering it when a neighbor who was working for a brokerage firm asked me, "Did you ever think about the stock market and becoming a broker?" Truly, I never had, even though I had an accounting background, and my husband and I owned a few stocks. But the more I thought about it, the more the idea appealed to me, so I began looking into brokerage companies in Center City, Philadelphia.

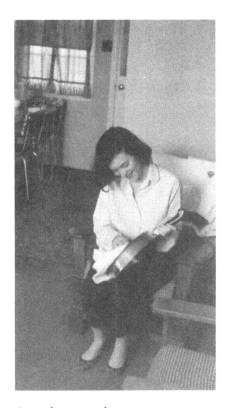

Being domestic early in our marriage.

Intrigued, I began to seriously consider this possibility. Never one to dilly-dally, I was soon interviewed by three firms. Two accepted me, and ultimately, I was hired by Robinson & Co. as a registered representative in the very new field of financial planning.

Only forty-five years before, women had finally won the right to vote in America in 1920. Although women had held jobs in the Spanish-American War overseas in France as telephone operators in the First World War in 1918 and as workers on factory lines during the Second World War, they still weren't a presence in many industries like finance in 1965. In my solidly middle-class neighborhood, all the men were professionals (like attorneys, physicians, accountants, and so on) who went to offices during the day while their wives either stayed at home taking care of the house and children, or worked nearby as teachers, receptionists, or administrative assistants. A sign of the times was that their career choices were far more limited than those of their husbands.

I cannot express how extraordinarily fortunate it was that Len always supported me in whatever crazy venture I dreamt up. He was even very encouraging of my working in Center City in the heart of downtown Philadelphia, which was extremely unusual in those days. I'd either take the train or drive about forty minutes so I could arrive at the office before the stock market opened at nine o'clock in the morning. It was not unusual for me to come home in the summer at around six in the evening, say a quick hello over the fence to my next-door neighbors whose children were in the pool, and then hurry into the house to enjoy dinner with my own family. It was important to me to try to be home for dinner most nights with my children, especially when they were young.

MARIE

Although I worked long hours and some days out of town, I was extremely fortunate to find, through an ad in the *Philadelphia Inquirer*, an unbelievable nanny to take care of our children and home. Marie was a beautiful African American woman who stood about five-foot, seven inches tall. Her hands were large, and she wore an ever-present smile. She had been born in Georgia, had picked cotton in the fields in her youth, and was a mother to nineteen grown children (eighteen with one man and one with another). With regard to motherhood, she'd say, "You put them in and you take them out."

Because Marie lived with us and was always in our home, I did not have to worry about the continuity of our children's care. She was very special and extremely devoted to each of them. Not only that, but she was also a favorite with all the neighborhood kids—especially when she'd hand out cookies by our garage door. And she also made the best mashed potatoes! Many times over the years, when our children were in elementary school, I'd find her reading their homework so that she herself could learn; with her upbringing, she had probably had very limited education, and perhaps she had not even gone to or finished high school.

She had a remarkable ability to discreetly disappear whenever we had guests. I can clearly remember her bringing out glasses of freshly squeezed lemonade on the patio when we had company and then just quietly retreating—she was never in the way. She embodied a type of old-fashioned refined discretion in the sense that she never interfered, hovered, or inserted herself as part of a situation. Instead, she was always present at the right moments to be helpful and supportive.

She had her own room on the lower level of our house, so she never disturbed us. In fact, she was so quiet and unobtrusive that when she broke her ankle one night, we had no idea until we arose the next morning. (To be clear, we considered her a part of the family and trusted her completely. And at the time, it was considered normal to sometimes employ live-in help of another race to serve in the home; I never gave such differences in race or ethnicity a thought.)

FAMILY FUN

My children tell me now that I was probably the tougher disciplinarian in our family than their father. (And I never called them "kids," since I considered the term demeaning; they were "children" or "human beings.") Len was a warm, affectionate father. By the time Karen, Kim, and Jeff reached their preteens, I knew that if anything were to happen to me, these three would be fine because of their sound minds and ethical values.

It was very important to me that we all celebrated holidays, birthdays, and successes together with both sides of our families, including our parents, siblings, cousins, nieces, and nephews. The Jewish holidays of Rosh Hashanah, Yom Kippur, Hanukkah, and Passover were observed either in our home on Bluebird Lane or at the home of Len's brother Sid and his wife Myrna. Early on, Myrna threw me a surprise bridal shower and since then, we've always remained very close.

Each child's birthday was celebrated in a special way, and I always tried to plan fun events with a twist: puppet shows for Karen, special-shaped cakes, twenty different cans of soda pop for Jeff, or a trip to the Philadelphia Zoo for Kim. There were too many to recount them all! We'd also hold celebrations at our local Howard Johnson's restaurant in Glenside. (Howard Johnson's, for readers who might not know, was a national hotel chain founded in 1925 that catered to families. It also had iconic restaurants all around the country that made it famous. Sadly, ours was replaced by a McDonald's in the 1970s. Today, only a single Howard Johnson's restaurant survives—in upstate New York.)

Our birth announcement of our first child, Karen Andre.

Every Mother's Day, if the weather permitted, we'd hold a celebration on our large back patio. On Halloween, Karen, Jeff, and Kim would go out trick-or-treating in their costumes while I stayed home to greet the neighborhood children. When I opened the front door, which was decorated with an old skeleton, I was wearing a scary mask that I pulled out of the closet every year. And on Sundays, after watching the Philadelphia Eagles football game, we'd go to Glenside Pizza for dinner. It was all great fun.

Len making merry with baby Karen.

All three of our children had either a bar mitzvah (for boys) or a bat mitzvah (for girls). This is a Jewish rite of passage wherein a boy or girl at the age of thirteen, after years of learning Hebrew and Jewish history, assumes the role of an adult. When they turned sixteen, all three of my children were confirmed at the same Reform Congregation Keneseth Israel near our home on Old York Road in Elkins Park.

In my early years when I worked for Robinson & Co., most of my appointments with my clients took place in the evening at their homes, when they tended to be most available. Remarkably for those conservative times, Len never objected to these evening visits. I'd come home from the office, have dinner with the entire family, and then head out to see clients. My oldest daughter Karen recently mentioned that she felt a bit funny when, in those early years, she was usually the only student whose mother did not pack their lunch.

Family portrait in 1973. Left to right: Me, Len, Kim, Jeff, and Karen.

Despite my early unorthodox career (more on that in Chapter 4), our family life was peaceful and orderly, not chaotic, thanks to the huge support from both Len and Marie. Len would bring groceries home from his small grocery store in north Philadelphia, which, as mentioned before, he held in partnership with his brother Sid. They became the fourth generation to work at this store; the sixth generation (Sid's boys and a grandson) is now running the business.

Because of the level of support I had on the domestic front, I truly never felt guilty that I was working, nor was I stressed about it. I was doing what I wanted to do and thoroughly enjoyed every minute of it.

KAREN ANDRE

Karen was born in Newport News, Virginia, at the Bon Secours Mary Immaculate Hospital in 1957, a six-and-a-half-pound, blonde, blue-eyed girl who emerged with very little hair and an overactive personality. By the time she was a year old, she was almost jumping out of her crib, and to this day she does not slow down, whether she's walking, talking, or running. She reminds me very much of Grandma Ida.

I recall her as a five-year-old, running out into the courtyard of our garden apartment and declaring, "Here I am, everybody!" Taking Karen shopping when

Karen being Karen with her usual unmistakable flair.

she was young was a trip in itself. It wasn't easy—but we managed, even with the opinionated voice that sometimes got a little loud in the dressing room of our local Strawbridge department store.

Karen and her sister Kim rarely argued as most sisters close in age usually do. They were and still are so different. Just as their looks are opposite, so are their personalities. However, they both love dogs and have my voice.

Karen was a voracious reader from an early age, with a quick mind and a love of travel. Living in suburban Dresher and attending the local schools, she was an excellent student, participated in the Girl Scouts, and was a cheerleader. She always had many friends, both male and female, and remains in touch with some of them from Upper Dublin High School. True to form, she always knew what she wanted—whether it was choosing to attend the University of Michigan, doing her senior college year in Kenya, or becoming a lawyer.

I recall Karen mentioning how she felt what discrimination was when she and another white student were booed on stage when she was in a play in Kenya. There, her ethnicity was the minority, and her skin color represented a complicated past in that country. It reminded me of my own first taste of racism's ugliness, as I related in Chapter 1, when my Black classmate Agnes and I were skipping arm in arm down the street at the age of eight in our Philadelphia neighborhood.

Karen has practiced as an attorney for more than three decades and has her own firm on Bainbridge Island in Washington State. Known for the quality of her legal work in criminal defense, business law, and employment issues, she is very well respected. Karen's sense of morals and ethics is above anyone else's that I have ever known. I used to joke that if I ever got into trouble with the law, Karen would be the first to not only pass judgment but also send me to jail—regardless that I'm her mother.

She is a deeply caring person with a love of country and community, and she's also an extremely loyal friend. She remains very much at the center of action on Bainbridge Island where we both live, whether it's politics or community affairs. In 2012, she ran for the position of Superior Judge in Kitsap County; although her campaign was excellent, I felt sad when she did not win.

Karen's son Ryan is my first grandchild. He was born on Bainbridge Island and started skiing with Karen and her husband John at the age of three. He is

Top: My sister-in-law Sharon and her daughter, Bari. Above: Karen, Ryan, and Len.

now a semiprofessional extreme skier, and Karen loves to watch him compete when she can. He is a very kind, gentle, talented, and intelligent young man.

Here is just one of the family stories often retold: One summer day when Karen was eleven, Kim nine, and Jeff seven, Len and I were out of town. After having a huge argument with Marie and with dogged willfulness, Karen grabbed her brother and sister and dragged them out of the house at the top of Bluebird Lane all the way down to the bottom of the hill. Then she proceeded to take them, with them crying all the way, to find their grandmother's home on Stenton Avenue. This was easily five miles, and I cannot imagine the scene of three young children, none very tall or stout, walking down the hill and into the city. It turned out that my mother was not at home when they arrived, so they had to walk another four blocks to find my brother Lew's home.

It wasn't until many years later that this tale finally came out. Determined, would you say, Karen was? Still is? As one of her many friends said, Karen is a force! But she's a very special woman and daughter who makes me proud.

Kim Susan

Kim was born in Philadelphia at the Einstein Medical Center in 1960. Kim's birth date was slated to be in March, but she was in no hurry to arrive. Concerned, I kept saying to myself in Yiddish, *koom shune*, which translates to "come soon." When Kim was finally born on April 4, I gave her the name Kim Susan, my close interpretation. Kim was two and a half years younger than Karen and a delightful child with long dark, curly hair, brown eyes, a shy smile, and a sweet disposition.

I remember one afternoon when I was outside our garden apartment and I came back in to find Kim, at the age of two, having completed one of her first artistic pieces—on our living room wall. Fortunately, this large display of colors was easily erasable. To this day, Kim is a talented artist. Her heart lies with the earth, and she's happiest when she's planting and tending to her extensive gardens.

As a child, she hated getting her thick, curly hair combed daily, as it tangled easily. Kim has always been extremely organized; she used to lay out the dress she'd wear to school the next day on her bed. She loved animals, especially her big, beautiful dog Sam, a shepherd-husky mix; I recall a lovely, detailed drawing of Sam that she completed in later years.

Kim had many friends, although she never hung out with her sister Karen's friends. She used to play with a little red-headed boy across the street as well as a girlfriend named Marjo and her brother who lived around the corner. She has a talent for languages and quickly conquered Hebrew, Spanish, and Italian. She was a very good student and probably the best musician of all my children; she took piano lessons at home during her childhood. I took two lessons myself and quickly

Kim (right) at the age of thirteen.

realized I had no talent, but Kim continued her training for a few years. She and Karen also did ballet after school on Mondays at Shirley Tratenberg's dance classes.

Kim eventually enrolled in Bennington, a very progressive private college in Vermont, but it was not the best school for her as it didn't fit her interests. (I probably would have liked to enroll there myself, as it was smaller, less structured, and offered more interesting classes than a typical college, and one could design their own course of study.) After her first year, she transferred to Hahnemann University in Philadelphia, where she majored in early childhood education. As a self-sufficient young woman, she found a small house to rent several blocks from the school. This forward-thinking entrepreneur then rented the house's other two bedrooms to students—and a couple of them became close friends with her for many years. Since I worked in town just a few blocks away, I enjoyed seeing her during the week.

After Kim graduated second in her class in 1983, Len and I gave her a graduation gift of a trip to Italy, Greece, and Israel, which she naturally organized herself. Ending up in Israel in a kibbutz near the Golan Heights, she fell in love with a recently discharged young soldier. With her talent for languages, including her fluency in Hebrew, Kim had no trouble communicating with Shahar and his parents in the kibbutz. Kim returned to the States with Shahar, and they lived in one of the apartments in a building I had developed, the Chocolate Factory. Shahar worked as a janitor at another of my buildings, the Castings, until they got engaged and went on a cross-country trip throughout America.

They eventually settled in Austin, Texas, and started planning a wedding. Therefore, it was a tremendous shock when I received a call from them on a late Saturday night in February 1991 to let me know that they had gotten married in Austin several months before. I was deeply saddened and hurt that I didn't get to attend their wedding.

Kim Yarden and her family at her daughter's wedding in 2022. From left to right: Batyah, Kim, Yehudit ("Didi"), Didi's husband Judah Jacobson, Shahar, and Shlomit.

Later, Kim and Shahar got involved in a fundamentalist Christian community that is now called Homestead Heritage. This group grew too large for the city of Austin and felt called to move to a new location in western Colorado. I later flew out there to see Kim and Shahar in their new community after she had a miscarriage. Over time, Homestead Heritage obtained a large parcel of land in Waco, Texas, and once again, Kim and Shahar relocated. I now have a close relationship with my very special daughter as well as many people in her Waco faith community.

I also have three very lovely granddaughters—Batyah, Yehudit ("Didi"), and Shlomit—all of whom Kim has homeschooled. They all read, write, and speak Hebrew in addition to English. It is a delight to spend time with them in Waco, where Kim is a loving wife, an excellent mother, a huge contributor to her community, and a caring, loving daughter.

JEFFREY SAMUEL

To meet Jeff is to meet a man with whom you feel his being immediately. Understated, handsome, and born blond but now turning gray, he is warm, friendly, energetic, and unique.

When we moved into our new home in Dresher in Philadelphia, Jeff was about a year old. When he was about two, we'd sometimes get a telephone call from a neighbor on Sunday mornings around 7 o'clock: "Your cute little boy is over at our house." Jeff, apparently half-asleep or sleepwalking, would get out our front door and wander over to our neighbor's house. Fortunately, this was a very safe, quiet,

Jeffrey in autumn 1964, at age two.

residential development with friendly neighbors. This occurred every so often for about six to eight months and then never again.

When Jeff was nine, he suffered a serious bout with viral encephalitis and was in the hospital for a few days. Then, when he was about eleven, he had meningitis, which also required a short hospital stay. Fortunately, our wonderful pediatrician Dr. Meyer diagnosed these infections very quickly, and Jeff did not suffer permanent damage. Both these infections are rare and can occur in children, but usually not in the same person.

Our Dresher house was an easy walk to Sandy Run Middle School, so Jeff was quite annoyed when I finally convinced his father to transfer him to a different school in eighth grade. William Penn Charter is a private, well-recognized Quaker boys school, and I felt the quality of education was better there. I had wanted to send our girls earlier to private schools, but the ever-practical Len was against them. I guess I'd worn him down by the time it came to Jeff, our youngest.

Jeff was an excellent athlete who led his track team, ran in Fairmount Park, and participated in the hurdles at Penn Charter's relay events. After graduating high school, Jeff chose to go to Tulane University in New Orleans. But after beginning his freshman year, he became uncertain as to whether it was the right engineering school for him. He came home frustrated and anguished on holiday break and while sitting in our dining room, decided to switch to Pennsylvania State University. He eventually graduated as a chemical engineer and today chairs the science department at a private school in Gates Mills, Ohio, near his home in Chagrin Falls. Not surprisingly, he's also the head track coach for the school's award-winning teams and coaches the basketball team for the local Special Olympics.

Nearing the age of sixty now, he still seemingly has every childhood friend he's made since nursery school. As a little boy, Jeff loved being with his friends, and they spent countless hours playing baseball, soccer, and football in our neighborhood. A loyal, incredibly generous soul, Jeff remains a part of their lives and even attends the bar and bat mitzvahs of their children.

A family portrait in the Chocolate Factory condo in Philadelphia around 1997. Left to right: Jeffrey, Shahar, Kim, me, my brother Lew (behind me), Jeff's wife Darla, and in the front, Batyah (Kim and Shahar's oldest daughter) and Nathaniel (Jeff and Darla's son).

Religion, family, and community are all extremely important to Jeff, as they are for me. He cares very deeply about family, friends, his students, and his gardens.

He is a father to a motivated son, Nathaniel, who is now twenty-six, as well as a special-needs daughter, Rebekah, who just turned twenty-one and is confined to a wheelchair due to a rare metabolic disorder that severely limits her muscle control and movement. Jeff makes every day special with the patience and care he gives to Rebekah, from teaching her to "turn the page, Rebekah" when they read a book together to staying up late each night preparing the food that she receives through a feeding tube. His devotion is nothing less than incredibly moving and awe-inspiring.

My own relationship with Jeff is very deep and very close. Every year without interruption over the past three decades before the COVID-19 pandemic, we would find a way to spend Kol Nidre together—the night before the holy day of fasting and Yom Kippur—no matter where he or I was living. We'd always spend these two special days together in a synagogue, whether it was in Philadelphia, Cleveland, Colorado Springs, Seattle, or Bainbridge Island, Washington. And even when we could not physically meet in the same city during the pandemic, Jeff and I still got together through Zoom.

A son of quality who gives tremendous love, kindness, and warmth, Jeff makes me swell with pride every day.

MARITAL DRIFTING

Sadly, but perhaps inevitably, with my days and evenings busy, the children growing up and eventually moving away to college, and our shifting life goals, Len and I gradually began drifting in different directions. After a major incident involving financing, I realized that my real estate development efforts were no longer of interest to Len. With my deep capacity for compartmentalizing projects, life, and work, I began to do more and more without his participation, almost without realizing what was happening to us.

Jeff's daughter Rebekah and me in 2019.

By the late 1980s, our children had graduated from college and were out of the house. Len decided to go back to Temple University to get his master's in social work. He and I were still living in the Chocolate Factory, a building I'd developed in Old City, but we were growing ever more distant as a team and a couple. After completing another all-consuming, fabulous historic renovation of a repurposed factory building, I went to visit Kim in Israel. When I arrived home, Len announced that he wanted a divorce after thirty-two years of marriage. I quietly agreed without arguing.

So, I thought it was a bit odd that shortly after this discussion, Len still wanted to go to our monthly bridge game with our old friends Fran and Dick at their house. This ritual had been going on for years, and we had not told anyone about our momentous decision. After all of us finished the game and we were having coffee and dessert, Len just blurted out without warning, "Florence and I are getting a divorce!"

Imagine the shock on the faces of our friends—and on my own.

4

TRAILBLAZING STOCKBROKER

Robinson & Co. ~ Dedication to Clients ~ Lessons Learned ~
Boardroom Aspirations ~ Attempts at Humiliation ~
Secrets to Success in a Man's World ~ Support at Home ~
Bankruptcy on the Horizon ~ Breaking into Bache ~
Gaining Institutional Clients ~ Kidder Peabody ~
Scary Florence ~ American Classic Financial ~ End of an Era

To begin to advise your client, know their risk level.
— Florence Klein —

As I related in the last chapter, I had never considered being a stockbroker until my neighbor mentioned it. But, with my accounting background and a desire for work that was both stimulating and promising economic advancement, I decided to investigate brokerage companies in Center City, Philadelphia. I interviewed with three firms, and soon I was on my way to a career that I never could have imagined.

ROBINSON & CO.

The final firm I intervicwed with was Robinson & Co., and it seemed more innovative than the first two. Located at the corner of Fifteenth and Chestnut streets—the vcry center of the city—Robinson was a small broker-dealer run by a quick-thinking son of one of the richest families in Philadelphia. This son, Bob Robinson, had the idea—which was very novel in 1965—to have a separate financial planning division. Even as president of the company, he conducted my interview himself and asked me what monetary goals I had for myself within a year's time. I quickly answered that $10,000 was realistic (equal to about $83,000 in today's dollars). He also had me take several personality and intelligence tests.

On June 1, 1965, at thirty-one years of age, married and with three young children at home, I became a member of Robinson & Co. I was thrilled by the prospect of working for a financial institution in a brand-new career field and even just coming to work in such a beautiful place. (The Robinson building was an iconic example of the many mid-century commercial office buildings in the very center of downtown Philadelphia in its heyday, with stores on the first floor and offices above. The building was owned by the wealthy Robinson family, well known for their automobile businesses and other ventures throughout Philly.)

Our company's financial planning programs had been developed by Murray Chotiner, an American attorney from Pittsburgh who had been a political mentor to President Richard Nixon. They were very well organized and contained sound client investment plans that are still commonly used today. But at the time, this was a groundbreaking approach for the investment world. Most firms like ours had been established by very wealthy investors who specialized in servicing the financial needs of their own privileged families and friends—such as the Morgans, the Rockefellers, and so on. These titans of business later branched out to serve the larger public population as opportunities arose, but most of these men making investments in real estate, private companies, and land still traded among themselves.

On May 17, 1792, twenty-four stockbrokers got together, so the story goes, under a buttonwood tree, and signed the Buttonwood Agreement outside of 68 Wall Street in Manhattan. This Agreement organized securities trading in New York City and would become the founding document of the first New York Stock Exchange.

I reference this history and the Buttonwood Agreement to give a flavor of the roots of the American finance industry and how it was only white men who monopolized it for many years. Even today, according to the *Women in Financial Services 2020* report, published by the international management consulting firm Oliver Wyman, women make up only about 20 to 23 percent of the higher echelons of financial management and investment services.

I must say that the initial training I received at Robinson & Co. was first-rate, thorough, and provided a meaningful background. It was headed by a very short, stout man named Albert, who sat on a high stool swinging his pulpy legs and was certainly very dismissive of me, Florence Klein. I was the only woman in the class and, as it turned out, the only woman in the firm besides Ruth, a secretary. I was so naive about the world of finance and brokerage firms that I did not think much about the fact that I was training to become possibly the very first female stockbroker in Philadelphia.

When Robinson & Co.'s financial planning division was being developed, its emphasis was on recommending mutual funds as the major investment vehicle. Mutual funds entered the American finance world in the 1890s, offering novice minor investors the opportunity to assemble a diversified portfolio of companies (whereas individual stock purchases represent a single company).

During my first six months with Robinson & Co., I learned not only about mutual funds but also about stocks, bonds, and options. I shadowed colleagues when they visited clients. Later I solicited my own clients, made appointments with them, and set up their mutual fund accounts. After about six months of training and passing the necessary exams, I became an officially registered broker.

DEDICATION TO CLIENTS

While still in training, I presented a new sales proposal: Set up small lunchtime seminars for women so they could gain more insight into the stock market. I felt that this might be a good way of attracting new clients and making personal finance more accessible to women. Over my seven years at the firm, I would host many such seminars. But Albert was not too happy about my getting such good grades and coming up with fresh new ideas so soon.

At the very beginning of my career, since I did not have high-net-worth relatives or friends whom I could approach, I mostly just cold-called people on the phone, asking for Mr. Smith or Jones (remember that these were the days before the Internet or email). I'd quickly introduce myself as a representative of the Philadelphia brokerage firm Robinson & Co. and ask whether they needed a college savings plan for their children. In this era, most married women were stay-at-home mothers caring for school-age children. I found that when these women heard a feminine voice on the phone, they wanted to know what I was calling about and why. They often hesitated a bit in their replies, and many times they'd ask me to call back when their husbands were home. (There were never unmarried "partners" in those days, nor were they free to make financial decisions entirely on their own.) Nonetheless, I was generally successful in arranging evening appointments in their homes.

These prospective clients often lived in the northeast section of Philly or in the nearby western suburbs. I'd ring the doorbells and the wives would answer. Invariably they were shocked when they opened their doors, only to see a young, very attractive, well-dressed woman by herself with no male colleague. After all, the only strangers who ever visited these row homes were the Fuller Brush salesmen or the Avon women who sold cosmetics. I'd confirm my affiliation with Robinson & Co., a fully licensed broker-dealer, and once I entered their homes, I'd immediately compliment them on their beautiful sofa or the color of their rugs as we went to the dining room table for my presentation. And their husbands, of course, would always join us.

Once we'd all sat down, I would emphasize that there was more to financial planning than just buying stocks, and I'd start each meeting with a series of questions. The first was to determine what their life goals might be; second, what their level of risk was; and third, if they had savings accounts to cover their basic living expenses for twelve to sixteen months. I'd also ask if they had wills and health

The former Robinson & Co. building where I worked (twelfth floor), first as a financial planner and later as a stockbroker. Built in the early 1900s, it was a commercial office building but is now apartments.

insurance. I'd inform them that there were no guarantees that their investments would not depreciate—and also that these *were* investments in their future. From their reactions, it was obvious that this was often the first time that they'd ever considered these questions.

During these meetings, I'd stress that these plans were personal to their specific needs and life goals and that everyone was different—and that they should not necessarily pursue what their neighbor might be investing in. It was important for them to understand that this was a serious commitment to their long-term financial security, not a competition or a lottery. I always helped them decide what their financial goals were and how to achieve them (and sometimes I'd already deduced what those might be before I even made appointments with them).

I always arrived extremely prepared, with plenty of suggestions at the ready. In these meetings, I took charge, directing the questions and listening to their responses, which mostly came from both the wife and husband in equal measure, although there were probably a few more from the men. Interestingly, I cannot remember any instances when the husband overrode the wife in making financial decisions, at least in front of me.

My clients were generally in their mid-thirties to fifties in age and were mostly middle-class. From the men who became clients during these home visits, I was able to obtain referrals to their friends and office colleagues. From these leads, I often earned new business from the companies they worked for or even their own businesses if they were entrepreneurs, although at this level, it was not traditional individual financial planning but working with the companies' pension plans.

Because most of my appointments took place in the evening after the dinner hour in various areas of the city and suburbs, Len insisted that I take our dog George along for protection in case somebody ambushed me near the car. George was a Weimaraner, and I'd leave him in the car during my appointments, which typically ran an hour to an hour and a half.

LESSONS LEARNED

Why was I attracted to the financial world? Foremost because it was interesting and a challenge. I quickly realized I could procure my own clients and successfully guide them to achieving their financial goals, which made me feel good since I was helping others who were not used to investing or even thinking about this level of life planning. I was genuinely interested in their objectives because finances touched every part of their lives, and I took their faith and trust in me very seriously.

Quality financial planning involves, of course, far more than just recommending or investing in stocks and bonds; it requires developing a personal plan that is tailored to the specific needs of a client and their family. It takes long-range thinking and good judgment because you're helping clients establish critical goals that truly determine the quality of the rest of their lives—and by extension, often those of their children when it comes to monetary reserves for illness, college, retirement, and vacation planning, as well as arranging legal connections for wills and insurance.

Just recently, a close friend's wife decided to pursue a new career in financial planning. She had already passed all the numerous exams necessary to engage with the public as a financial advisor, and she was keenly interested in any advice I could give her. Needless to say, I was happy to dig deep into my mind and memory to dredge up some knowledge and experience that would help her.

Looking back, I do wish now that I would have had a mentor whom I could have called upon. It's perfectly okay to be a solitary trailblazer, but it helps immensely to also have guides who can help you avoid pitfalls and embarrassing mistakes.

I remember being invited once to a local women's meeting in my suburban neighborhood of Fort Washington. After I was pleasantly received, they wanted me to join their organization, which was trying to rebuild this very old area called Ambler, and they gave me a list of their members. I was just getting started at Robinson & Co. and was anxious to find new clients. After a day or so, I started calling these women to ask about financial planning and to set up appointments with them. Their quick, negative replies delivered quite coldly soon made me realize that I shouldn't have been so aggressive with this new list. It was a lesson learned early!

BOARDROOM ASPIRATIONS

After working at Robinson & Co. for two and a half years, I was becoming quite successful at financial planning. Not only was I getting my own clients and setting up a steady stream of lunch seminars, but I was also becoming keenly interested to work downstairs in the boardroom, not just in the financial planning department.

One day I approached the department manager, Al Pitts, to tell him about my interest in the boardroom, which was still populated only by men. After all, I now had some experience, held all the necessary licenses, and was performing well for the company. But I still wanted to be in the thick of the action and to have the same advantages as all the other stockbrokers.

Al's answer was swift. "Oh no, Florence—why would you want to go into the boardroom and get involved with stocks and bonds? You know that is really more risk-oriented, and, besides, you're doing so well now. The market is so volatile."

A few weeks later, I again requested to make the move and received the same negative reply. Of course, that didn't stop me. I went to Frank, the boardroom manager, and requested the new role. Frank's response was the same denial. At first, he tried to dissuade me by making the same allusions to the daily changes in the stock market and suggesting that concentrating on financial planning might be a much better fit for me. Both Al and Frank then avoided me for the next few weeks, but I quietly and assertively made my request again. Once more, it was denied.

Al was a young, pleasant man of around thirty-five years of age, quick to smile and wink; he seemed to be happy working for this innovative new division in the company. Frank, on the other hand, was an old hand, having been a stockbroker for most of his forty-five or so working years. He was extremely knowledgeable, quick-speaking, and fast-thinking—and totally dedicated to helping the men under his command.

Three weeks later, I made my request yet again. Perhaps they were surprised at my persistence. I felt certain that they were not dismissing me, exactly—they just wanted to make sure I kept up my productivity and weren't certain I could handle the pressure. After all, they had never overseen any women brokers before.

Completely undeterred when I had an objective, I continued pursuing my wishes until the managers finally understood that, with my positive work performance, I could easily transfer to another brokerage firm. They consented to give me a desk directly in front of the large moving stock exchange tape. At last, I'd made it into the boardroom with the other stockbrokers! I was thrilled.

Still, I did not consider this a promotion. There was no change in my title or my salary, which was based entirely on commissions. But I did not want to limit myself—here were opportunities for more clients, more diverse sectors (such as larger companies), and more products. And why not? I had earned all the necessary licenses, worked hard, and produced for myself and the firm. I also wanted the chance to speak to the men in this boardroom and learn from their experience and knowledge.

Exactly what did this much-coveted room look like? Well, a very large board was affixed to the front wall of the office, and at the bottom of it was a teleregister that transmitted the opening, current, and closing prices of various stocks as flashing numbers in a moving picture across it. There were probably thirty-five of us—all men except me—and we all sat at desks relatively close to one another, with no partitions between us. The room was very plain, with no decorations or windows, which was par for the course for a small firm at the time.

This boardroom's utterly ordinary atmosphere gave no outward indicators that my colleagues "had arrived," so to speak—and I certainly did not think I "had arrived" either.

A little bit of history here: I remember the moment I first heard about the bankruptcy of the Penn Central Transportation Company while sitting in front of this stock exchange board. This was a major shock, as the venerable company, which was founded in 1846 as Pennsylvania Railroad in Philadelphia, had become not only the biggest railroad less than four decades later, but also the single largest corporation in the world, with a budget second only to that of the US government. Pennsylvania Railroad absorbed the New York Central in 1968 and the New Haven & Hartford Railroad in 1969 to form the famous Penn Central, but two years later, the entire company collapsed due to a series of unfortunate circumstances. Some may recall that its new name post-bankruptcy became Conrail, and we now know its consolidated passenger service operations and railroad lines as Amtrak.

At the time, Penn Central's bankruptcy made most people in the finance world as well as average citizens very concerned. Any time that such a large, long-standing public institution previously thought to be reputationally solid and a financial giant has to enter bankruptcy, it rattles people. There was an expectation back then that being so enormous always meant safety and security, but as we know now, that just isn't true. We've been rocked globally by numerous major bankruptcies after the 2008 fall of the stock market, more recent market volatility, and the introduction of new types of investments such as special purpose acquisition companies (SPACs).

ATTEMPTS AT HUMILIATION

At the time I gained access to the boardroom at Robinson & Co., we were all called stockbrokers. The normal practice at my firm was that a designated broker was assigned to be "broker of the day." If a potential client came wandering off the street into our office—a rarity since we were on the fifteenth floor and did not have many walk-in clients—that broker would have the first opportunity to serve them.

On one Tuesday, I was the broker of the day (for the first time ever) when a very petite Black woman came in. She wanted to sell some municipal bonds that she had inherited from her uncle. (Municipal bonds are issued by states, counties, and utilities as opposed to the corporate bonds that companies issue. In the 1960s—long before home computers, the Internet, and electronic financial systems were available to the general public—people often had physical stock-and-bond paper certificates that were issued in their own name, which they kept in their homes or in a safe deposit box at their bank.)

I discussed the transaction with this woman, took down her personal information, and was pleased to have a new client. The transaction was for $55,000 (municipal bonds are sold in denominations of $1,000). A bond issued by the state that paid 5 percent interest and matured in 1980 would today be worth $173,000 ($100 in 1980 is worth $360 today in 2022).

It turned out that Mrs. Breward would become a loyal client for many years.

After she left the office, I filled out the trade tickets and proceeded to walk to the back of the office to turn them in to Mike Kinsella, the trader. His station was behind a high walnut platform above the boardroom, so he had a clear view of the entire area where about thirty-five male brokers worked. I turned in the tickets and walked back to my desk. No sooner had I sat down when a booming voice yelled "KLEIN!"

I quickly strode to the front of the trading desk and stood looking up at Mike. He then proceeded to loudly berate me, bellowing, "What is *THIS* you gave me? Don't you know how to fill out a trading form? What is WITH you?!"

His thunderous voice reverberated throughout the open room. I stood there, me at all of five feet, three and a half inches—maybe five feet, six inches with my heels—listening to this ugly, embarrassing harangue. I said not a word. I just listened to his outburst and thought to myself, *I AM GOING TO MAKE IT—IN SPITE OF YOU AND BECAUSE OF YOU!!! I DID MAKE IT!*

Once I spoke those silent words to myself, I knew right then that neither he nor anyone else was ever going to stop me.

Mike expected me to burst out crying, which of course I did not. My first thought as I heard his fury was that he obviously did not appreciate a woman in the boardroom, and he wanted to completely humiliate me in front of all my male colleagues. Traders are generally not known for having passive personalities and are under constant, intense pressure to make decisions quickly in volatile markets. Within minutes or even seconds, the stock or bond positions they're working on may scuttle away from the price they're attempting to buy or sell at. It takes a certain personality and temperament to do this job.

After fifty-six years, I can still hear Mike's voice.

I never mentioned this incident to anyone. No one came up to me after I sat back down at my desk. I didn't discuss it with any of the managers. Needless to say, I never received any assistance from my male colleagues—and I never expected any. I already knew that they did not appreciate my ideas, innovative approaches, and hard work. Many of them took long lunches and leisurely happy hours and were not truly interested in increasing their client lists.

SECRETS TO SUCCESS IN A MAN'S WORLD

Does this sound like a hard way to get started in what everyone thinks is an exciting career? Truly, I did not feel it was difficult because fortunately, I've been blessed with positive energy most of my life. In fact, it motivated me even more to make a success of my new career.

And I believe I became successful at Robinson & Co. because I set rules for myself: I was a professional, a woman, and a mother. Proper appearance, decorum, and manners were very important to me; for instance, I wore a hat every day (it became my signature, even today). My own personal rules governed how I conducted myself—I never went out to lunch with the male brokers for whom martinis were their regular drink, or to after-hours get-togethers or dinner with them. I did not expect any preferential treatment from my bosses or colleagues, nor was I in the industry to make friends.

I felt no desire to engage in extra activities with any of my clients either—it was just a part of setting my own boundaries in the early years. (Although on later occasions I did have to take some of my clients—especially those affiliated with the larger institutional accounts—out to lunch, dinner, or the occasional Broadway show as part of my work duties—it was common, expected practice with that higher level of clientele.) But I always keenly understood that my primary purpose was to understand their financial risk levels and goals and be responsive to their needs.

I also never asked for help in getting new clients. At the time, most stock-brokers came from families who had long-standing relationships with their own brokers or knew someone in the family like an uncle or a grandfather with some wealth and knowledge of investments. But I had no such connections; my parents were on a lower socioeconomic level. Thus, I had to find and develop all my own clients from scratch, and I worked hard to earn them.

As time went on, most of my clients with larger portfolios were men, simply because they held higher positions and were ready and able to invest larger amounts of money. I never felt that my success was due to my having a softer "woman's touch"—perhaps I was simply more perceptive of my clients' needs and emotions, and I listened well.

It also helped that I saw opportunities in many of my new connections and wasn't afraid to seize them when they presented themselves. One day, I was meeting with a client when he started discussing the Philadelphia Teachers' Credit Union. It rang a bell with me since I'd previously worked for them when I was in eighth grade. I called the credit union, met with its financial department—and then it became a client, just like that. In fact, it was the first of many credit unions that would later become clients of Robinson & Co. and other firms I worked for.

Today there are many more female financial advisors and even ones running their own investment firms. But this was not so in the 1960s when I began. In the 1970s, women began to be treated more fairly as they earned more financial compensation for themselves and their companies (mostly from commissions on sales). As women moved into management positions, however, they were given titles but once they got closer to top management, they were usually met with silent, powerful objections from the male-dominated firms. Many examples exist of very talented, strong-willed, intelligent women who sued numerous brokerage firms for gender discrimination—and many more who unfortunately lost their suits. I hope to talk about some of these women in another book someday.

And, in case you wondered about Mrs. Breward, the Black woman who came into Robinson & Co. to sell her municipal bonds: It was indeed a little unusual to see a Black person walk into an office like ours in those days, as not many clients visited us in the first place. Her ethnicity was no big deal to me, as I had spent my childhood in several neighborhoods where larger Black populations lived, especially near Temple University on Broad Street. But, as you might recall, I also grew up welcoming all kinds of people, regardless of their ethnicity or skin color.

SUPPORT AT HOME

Of course, as I've said before, I was extraordinarily fortunate to have amazing support at home for my burgeoning career from my husband and Marie, our wonderful live-in housekeeper and nanny. In those days, most women simply did not hold professional positions if they were married and had children. If they did work outside the home, they were usually limited to socially and culturally accepted female positions as teachers, travel agents, librarians, clerks, secretaries, nurses, and administrative assistants. While some could set the hours they worked and be at home when their children returned from school, many could not, and their children were sometimes labeled as "latchkey kids." This added to the social stigma often suffered by working mothers.

This may sound odd to younger readers now, but it was unheard of at the time for a professional woman to meet with clients in the evening. No one I knew did this, except for insurance salespeople—but they were all men, as women did not work in this industry until more recently. In this regard, Len was especially supportive of me; he was such an unusual husband for 1965. Fifty-seven years ago, very few men and certainly none of our friends' husbands would have ever permitted their wives to visit clients after-hours, let alone take them to New York City for dinner and a show and be away from home overnight (in separate hotel rooms, of course). Such a thing was just not done, as it suggested impropriety in that more socially conservative, restrictive era. That said, Len might mention that I was working too hard or putting in such long hours, but he also understood the demands of my career and what I needed to do to advance it. Some men even today might have difficulty with this arrangement, but the trust between me and Len was always unquestioned and unspoken.

Because Len was in the family retail grocery business with his brother Sid, he was able to schedule his days off, which was also extremely unusual at the time. That allowed more flexibility in our home life and child-rearing. And my children adored Marie for the six years she worked for us, and they all seemed well-adjusted, knew they were loved, and accepted our unusual household as normal.

BANKRUPTCY ON THE HORIZON

In the late 1960s, demand for new stock issues arose from young companies that wished to go public. In those days, for a company to raise additional capital in the public market, it needed to hire an investment banker from a major firm (usually Goldman Sachs, Bache Halsey Stuart Shields, Morgan Stanley, or J.P. Morgan) to underwrite the new company stock issue, arrange for other investment companies to participate, and bring it public on the New York Stock Exchange or the American Stock Exchange on a date set by the firms.

A photo of me that ran in Philadelphia *magazine in April 1977. At this time, I was working for Bache Halsey Stuart Shields, specializing in government securities. The caption read, "Hats are my trademark. I've always worn them and have a closetful in all colors and shapes. I can add a hat to a simple skirt, sweater, and scarf and I look finished. I never wear slacks to work; I never have. I'm interested in how I look totally, and dresses, suits, or ensembles give a better all-over feeling. Generally I dress conservatively because that's what I think my clients expect. It's important to be well-dressed. You are better received when you walk into an office."*

This had been the usual procedure for new issues until around 2015—that was when the process of a company going public changed. Now, as of 2022, it seems as though protocols are changing every day. Many companies are bringing themselves to the public market without going through traditional investment bankers, who charge high transaction fees. One very new method becoming popular today involves the special-purpose acquisition company, or SPAC, which is a shell corporation created to collect funds to finance a merger or an acquisition within a certain timeframe. Because an SPAC may be listed on the stock exchange, this eliminates the usual need to undergo an initial public-offering process.

But Robinson & Co., at the time I was working for it, was a small firm with only one office in Philadelphia. They did not usually get what's known in the industry as "new issue allocations," nor did they have a dedicated department or the personnel to pursue this business. To this day, I marvel that I had the guts to walk into the venerable New York office of Lehman Brothers, a large, well-known brokerage firm with a very active investment department that specifically solicited new companies to become public. Sitting down with its new-issue department head, I described my firm Robinson & Co. and requested an allotment of a specific set of stocks that I knew would be coming to the market soon. When the issue was released, Robinson received a small distribution of the shares, and both its managers and other brokers were quite surprised. Naturally, this did not particularly endear me to my colleagues at Robinson, who weren't looking to expand business with many new or innovative ideas. But my strategy worked, and I was able to secure quite a few new-issue distributions over the next several years.

Trouble was brewing, however. Unbeknownst to any of us outside of top management, Robinson had a collateral shortage. To explain: For any company to be a licensed broker-dealer, it is required to maintain a set amount of funds and report those totals monthly to prove that it is fully prepared to service its clients and still hold a comfortable percentage in reserves, according to the National Association of Securities Dealers (NASD). The NASD sets these amounts according to the monetary totals of the clients being serviced; other regulations must be followed as well.

In 1972, we brokers had no idea that there was a problem until we were told by a manager that our firm would be closing in ten days. To say that this was a shock was an understatement of the greatest magnitude. Imagine how Bob Robinson felt, the son of the titular head of this powerful family and the president of the company. I believe that many members of his family had invested heavily in the firm. By this time, I'd been with Robinson & Co. for seven years.

I quickly landed an interview with Bache Halsey Stuart Shields, one of the first firms I had interviewed with in 1965. They were very happy to hire me—not so much because I was a woman but because I was bringing my lucrative clientele from Robinson with me. I transferred my licenses to Bache Halsey Stuart Shields and got to work.

BREAKING INTO BACHE

Bache Halsey Stuart Shields was an old-line Chicago-based firm with many offices in New York City. Our Philadelphia office was situated in an odd location above a Woolworth's five-and-dime store on Chestnut Street, not far from the Robinson building (most brokerage firms at the time were in traditional office buildings that may not have housed retail stores).

From a photo shoot. My real life wasn't quite this glamorous.

One evening, I stayed late in the office after all the men—there were still no women brokers in Philly in 1972—had left the building and the elevator was locked for the night. I had to wind my way down the fire escape from the third floor. How funny and odd I must have looked coming out into an alley with my hat, suit, and heels! I didn't do that again.

Our office was a large square room with three rows of desks spaced relatively close together. One day, I noticed a small group of men seated on the left side of the room who seemed to be talking intensely among one another. Ever curious, I spotted another man sitting nearby—I think his name was Nathan—and I asked him, "What are those men working on?" Nathan replied that they were institutional brokers—the ones who handled large companies and institutions.

By that time, I had been working at my usual high level at BHSS to develop clients and produce revenues (all on commission) for about nine months or so. I spotted my chance. I asked to speak to my manager Jack Petroskey, a very pleasant man.

"I would like to call on savings and loan associations and other institutional clients," I told him, brightly.

His response was immediate. "Florence, that is not for you!" he retorted.

This sounded familiar. But I did not question him. In fact, I told him that I understood that "women were not institutional brokers."

Of course, it was taken for granted at BHSS and probably at the majority of similar firms that only men were institutional brokers—because they were. I never discussed the issue with my colleagues or managers. But since I was never one to be told no for a reason that didn't make any sense to me, I quietly decided right then and there that I, myself, and Florence would try developing my own institutional accounts. Using just a pen, a phone, and my brand-new, trusty yellow legal pad, I started calling on savings and loan associations (S&Ls) throughout Pennsylvania. I researched the types of investments that these institutions could and could not invest in, since they were highly regulated. And because most of the S&Ls were small, I was successful.

Since many readers may not be familiar with S&Ls, which are uncommon these days, let me give you a little background. Many of them were created in the early twentieth century as a friendlier, more community-oriented means of assisting people with home ownership and passbook savings accounts versus the bigger, impersonal banks. (I myself had such a passbook when I was in the third or fourth grade; every week or so, I'd go to my local S&L and deposit two dollars.) The S&Ls of this early era were also portrayed in the iconic 1946 film *It's a Wonderful Life*.

Most S&Ls sprang up during the Great Depression in 1929 when it was difficult for the average person to obtain financing for a home; the Federal Reserve helped by establishing the Federal Home Loan Bank. S&Ls were originally quite limited as to whom they could lend to or what services they could provide—for instance, they did not offer personal checking accounts until the 1980s. As a broker, I was able to work with them, since I understood their requirements and what government obligations they could purchase from a regulated firm like BHSS. I called on them in person and within about a year or two, I had garnered many of the S&Ls in the state of Pennsylvania as my accounts. So, I guess I was now an institutional broker—except that I was never actually *assigned* a single institutional account!

Because of various state-level cases of abuse, fraud, and other problems, the number of S&Ls declined over the ensuing years. Tighter regulations developed in the late 1980s, and now, in 2023, government-backed Freddie Mac and Fannie Mae hold the bulk of responsibility for housing mortgages in America.

GAINING INSTITUTIONAL CLIENTS

BHSS later moved to a more conventional office building in Philadelphia. As my production increased, I earned a vice presidency. After that, Jack pretty much left me alone and I now had the approval to find institutional clients who were not being covered by other brokers. But there was one issue: Most of those accounts are assigned by the sales manager of a firm—who—you guessed it—are men. Even after I became a vice president, I was still never officially assigned a single account.

Despite this, I still tremendously enjoyed the business and challenge of pursuing and opening new government accounts, which included interacting with many men in government positions throughout Pennsylvania, Maryland, and Washington, DC. This often involved traveling to DC and staying overnight at the Watergate Hotel (and this was just after the resignation of President Nixon). I once bought a lovely blouse from that hotel's gift shop, plus I enjoyed many memorable moments in DC during my many trips. And I still have the blouse!

Along with my S&L and government clients, I added credit unions and municipal accounts. As with Robinson & Co., all these clients were ones whom I called and developed relationships with myself. How did I do this? As I related earlier in this chapter, in the very early days, I'd write down the names of prospects on my thirty-six-line yellow pad and make cold solicitation calls by telephone. And as we know, it's always the last one on the list who'd respond favorably. I'd then make appointments to meet with that person and thus was able to add them to my client list without any introduction by the firm. (To explain: Such introductions weren't actually required, but most large commercial banking and government accounts were handled only by institutional brokers, who were in turn heavily influenced by their investment firms. This way of conducting business called for plenty of socialization, so my colleagues would end up playing golf and going to ball games with their all-male clients. In fact, I cannot recall having any institutional clients who were women, whether they were affiliated with private companies, credit unions, S&Ls, government agencies, or labor unions.)

How did I become so successful in this competitive business? For one thing, I was able to develop accounts that weren't really sexy. They didn't garner responses like, *Oh wow, you just bagged a big-name bank or large corporation*—these were generally less flashy, overlooked accounts. But these clients nonetheless appreciated that I was experienced, knew what I was doing, and didn't recommend stock issues that weren't appropriate. I was gutsy, followed through on a regular basis, and was genuinely interested in helping these men (yes, still mostly men even in the 1980s).

I also made it a rule to always be guided by the client and their needs, whether it was an individual, a credit union, or a municipality. I simply understood that what they needed was not necessarily the biggest trade, and I always made sure to know what risk level my clients were comfortable with and not violate those boundaries.

KIDDER PEABODY

In 1979, when I was forty-five years old, I began getting calls from the prestigious investment banking firm of Kidder, Peabody & Company to join them. After negotiating for about a year and enticed by a comfortable incentive, I began working for them, where I had my own office and secretary. By then, another woman was working as a broker in the trading side of the office who, as I remember, was very involved in meditation and healthful eating (ahead of her time).

TICKER TAPE

My customer's man is a lady,
And, fellow investors, I'm glad;
I no longer figure and worry
Like when I bought stocks from a lad.

She recommends General Motors,
American, Chrysler and Ford;
I buy one, then go in and watch her,
While others are watching the board.

If you, too, are playing the market,
But find you're enjoying it less,
You know what'll perk up your gusto?
A customer's man in a dress!

I sometimes included this playful poem in notes and holiday cards to clients.

I easily recall my introduction to the firm of KP on a cold Philly day because of its uniqueness. I was greeted by the tall, regal Thomas L. Ashbridge III, a very distinguished gentleman. He was always impeccably dressed in a suit, as were all the men. Even on the last day of the workweek, no one at KP would dare even think to dress casually on Fridays, a trend that started in the 1980s. A lifelong devotee to equestrian sports, Thomas was a master of foxhounds. He'd been the office manager at KP for several years before becoming an investment banker for the company.

I was characteristically attired in my proper business suit and hat when he greeted me warmly and explained that KP had a traditional practice of introducing new investment brokers to the firm's staff. Mr. Ashbridge (I never called him Tom) then proceeded to walk me down the hall to the boardroom where most of the brokers were sitting at their respective desks. Here I am, the first woman—and Jewish at that—with her own private office and secretary. It was quite a bit for Mr. Ashbridge to swallow.

"Florence, I would like to introduce you to John Wells Green, Jr. His father is from the Wellesley family and his mother's family came over to the US in the 1770s. Next, Florence, I would like to introduce you to Wilbur J. Kroger; he sits on the family board. And here is John V. McPherson—his brother is the CEO of one of the major beverage companies and one of the best polo players in the state of Florida."

These introductions continued through at least ten or fifteen more men. No mention was made of my background or what caused KP to invite me to join the firm. It was a very memorable morning, to say the least. I am certain that if Mr. Ashbridge had still been the office manager, he would not have hired me. I do recall, however, his inquiring about my children and who was caring for them, even though it was not a politically correct question to ask an employee.

It turned out I'd have very few conversations with him while working at KP. However, Raymond Welsh, the manager of the Philadelphia office, was known for his astute grasp of the stock market and for being a very generous, philanthropic person with a pleasant personality. Over the ensuing years, Ray provided me with many opportunities even though I remained the only female investment banker with the company.

At KP, I grew my client portfolio to include federal government agencies, the City of Annapolis, and major labor unions. This earned me a full vice presidency, which was quite an accomplishment. In contrast to Robinson & Co. and its inability to acquire new stock issues for its clients, KP was a major player in bringing new companies public. I was asked to research emerging business opportunities, such as windmills in California or new boats on the Mississippi River. There were also introductions to various companies for which KP would serve as the lead underwriter or a major firm in underwriting new issues.

Sometimes we'd hold private hearings with other investment firms to discuss and promote new opportunities for our clients. These meetings took place at the very elite Union League of Philadelphia on Broad Street, a short walk from our office. The Union League was built in 1865 as a quasi-secretive men's club and established during the Civil War to promote loyalty to the newly elected President Abraham Lincoln, who did indeed visit many times. Not surprisingly, the Union League refused to admit women as members until 1986, nor did it allow a female president of its board until—would you believe it—2010.

As an investment banker, I was invited to participate in these meetings. However, because absurd traditions die hard, women had to be specially invited to the premises and even then, they could enter only through the less conspicuous Fifteenth Street entrance, not the stately Broad Street one. The first time I attended a meeting here, I walked in through the Fifteenth Street entrance and took the elevator to the third floor. After the meeting ended, I decided to walk down the building's hallowed interior marble steps. (I have always loved beautiful, old buildings and adored feeling their aura of history deep in my psyche.)

As I descended these majestic stairs to the elegant first floor, a Black usher in uniform stood at the bottom, watching me with a look of utter amazement on his face. He was literally speechless—*how on earth had I gotten in? Who was I?* He was too stunned to ask these questions, and I helped him by gently saying, "I have just

The venerable Union League of Philadelphia, with its famous, magnificent stairway out front.

attended a meeting on the third floor with Kidder Peabody." Imagine—how did I have the gumption to enter the building, let alone stroll down its wide spiral staircase with its magnificent wood balustrades and polished copper maidens holding up the glittering lightbulbs?

Since I sometimes invited clients out to lunch, we might dine at the Union League or go there when we had a conference. They were usually quite impressed.

SCARY FLORENCE

One year, a credit union convention took place in a hotel for Pennsylvania members in Pittsburgh. As the hostess, I was dressed in a smashing black cashmere long skirt and top, one of my favorite outfits. It was an enjoyable event attended by about seventy-five men and a few women. Although I never ate or drank much at these functions, I was tired by the end of the evening. I went up to my room and closed and locked my door.

Fifteen minutes later, I heard a knock.

"Florence, it's Tony." He was the manager of one of the credit unions. "I know you're exhausted. Let me massage your feet since you've been standing in the room all afternoon in your high heels."

Not opening the door, I calmly said, "Oh, thanks, Tony, I'm fine, just a bit tired. See you in the morning."

Tony tried again to persuade me to let him in, but I did not open the door. I hadn't expected this, but I wasn't afraid either. After he walked away, I thought about how I was to face him in the morning without making him feel uncomfortable. The next day, I saw him at breakfast, smiled, and never said another word about the incident. Fortunately, Tony was still pleasant to me when I spoke to him about credit union financial suggestions. He had been persistent, but so was I.

When I heard in 2007 that the famous Drake Hotel in New York City was being torn down and demolished, it brought back a memory of another incident. This was when I was working at KP, and I was going into NYC to take an institutional client out to see *Gentlemen Prefer Blondes* at the legendary Majestic Theatre. I boarded an Amtrak train from the Thirtieth Street Station in Philadelphia and arrived at about eleven in the evening with my small suitcase. I had worked late that day and was exhausted. Hopping into a taxi, I asked the driver, "Would you mind dropping me off at a drugstore and waiting for me?" NYC is one of those special cities with drugstores that are open twenty-four hours.

The cab driver did wait for me and then we proceeded to the Drake. But instead of taking me to its front entrance, he let me off at its side door. I smiled to myself; apparently, the taxi driver had just assumed I was one of the "girls of the night." You never know what people might think of you—especially when you need to stop at a drugstore and then at a hotel at a very late hour.

Throughout my career in finance, it simply never crossed my mind that I could not compete or work with my male colleagues, nor at any time did I ever feel inadequate to do the work. The #MeToo events of 2017 and 2018, with the exposure of Harvey Weinstein and so many other men who sexually took advantage of the women who worked for them, gave me pause to question: Why did none of the men in Robinson & Co., where I was probably the first female stockbroker in Philadelphia, ever approach me? No man ever touched me, intimidated me, or even suggested interest in a date, lunch, or anything else. I wondered why. I was young, well-built, and beautiful, with a pleasant personality.

Many years later, I asked my grown son Jeff about this. Without hesitating, he answered, "Oh Mom, they were scared of you!" I also asked a dear cousin the same question and her answer mirrored Jeff's: "You were always so sure, so together, that no man would ever think of coming toward you."

Really, was my astonished thought—I did not think I was *that* scary!

But it is true that I didn't want or invite such attention, and I think men could sense this from my business demeanor and professionalism; they quickly realized that they weren't going to get anywhere with me if they tried. It reminded me of my high school days when boys always wanted to be around me, but they knew they couldn't target me sexually—I was too much of an ice queen even then and perhaps too self-confident for them to even try. I wasn't easy prey, and thus they didn't try to take advantage of me. Tony, of course, was interested in me, but he may have also had a bit too much to drink at that annual conference. I must say that it was quite unusual—the only time I recall ever being approached inappropriately during my career. I suspect that one advantage I had was that I did not directly depend on any man for my job or production—I made my own contacts and was careful to not put myself in difficult situations.

AMERICAN CLASSIC FINANCIAL

While I was completing my degree in management from the Wharton School in the late 1970s, I met a fellow student who suggested looking into forming our own firm. By now, I was primarily handling large institutional clients at Kidder Peabody. The year I graduated was 1979, and quite a year it was. Not only had I been in college that year but so was the rest of our family—my daughter Karen at the University of Michigan, daughter Kim at Bennington College, son Jeff at Penn Charter, and husband Len getting his master's in social work from Temple University in Philadelphia.

In 1984, I was able to place a large corporate bond issue with another broker-dealer, and I decided to move my investment licenses to a different firm called Gruntal & Company. As a result, I was no longer working at the prestigious KP when it was purchased by General Electric Company in 1986. This takeover turned out not to be positive for KP; its nimble, entrepreneurial style typical in brokerage firms clashed with that of staid, bureaucratically corporate GE. Subsequently, the 115-year-old Kidder Peabody was sold again and now sadly is no more.

Although my new firm Gruntal had guaranteed when I signed on with them that they could handle my institutional clients, it turned out they weren't equipped to service them after all. I then investigated purchasing a small mainline firm in Bryn Mawr on Lancaster Avenue. This firm specialized in mutual funds, which I knew quite well from my days at Robinson & Co. I incorporated the name American Classic Financial, completed all the numerous additional licenses for operating a national financial firm in 1988, and thus became one of the few woman-owned,

AMERICAN CLASSIC GROUP

American Classic Development Company

American Classic Financial Company

American Classic Management Company

Classic Properties International

AMERICAN CLASSIC
FINANCIAL COMPANY

Executive Office:

53 North Mascher Street
Philadelphia, PA 19106
215/238-0220

355 E. Lancaster Avenue, Haverford, Pa. 19041

106 Society Hill
Cherry Hill, New Jersey 08003

licensed broker-dealer firms in the United States. A year later, I opened a second ACF office in the Castings, one of the major buildings I developed.

My original plan was to continue working with my existing various large institutional accounts and hire other stockbrokers to handle other accounts. But one cannot always plan for the positive. In the early 1990s, the Federal Reserve changed many of the collateral requirements necessary for transactions involving government securities as well as trading rules. We were too small to compete in this arena, and even though I so enjoyed this type of business, I simply couldn't continue servicing all the institutional clients I had accumulated over the years. This was very sad for me, and it foretold the closure of my firm.

END OF AN ERA

In 1998, I met a man named Larry Karlin and moved with him to Colorado Springs. I had intended to relocate my firm and hire other brokers there, but after checking the qualifications of available applicants in the area, I decided not to. This turned out to be a wise decision as the public was turning its attention to penny stocks and more speculatory areas that were becoming all the rage in the market, and those were not sectors that I knew or preferred.

American Classic Financial stayed operating for a few more years. After a simple overlooked legal form caused unbelievable difficulties, I closed the firm, and my long, groundbreaking career in finance came to an end after forty years.

5

COURAGE

**How Do We Be Brave? ~ Being Grateful ~
Taking a Stand to Help Others ~
Being Brave in the Workplace ~ Courage in Prison**

Courage is more exhilarating than fear, and in the end, it is easier.
— *Eleanor Roosevelt* —

Courage is a trait we could all use more of. It's not always what we think about when we hear the word, such as the bravery summoned during a heroic rescue or a dramatic mission. But in fact, it simmers and manifests in the biggest and smallest of ways within all of us—often when we're not even aware of its quiet but steady presence.

What is courage, exactly? I believe that courage is understanding yourself, having the plain old guts to go forward and not stop. It requires taking the time to get to know yourself as a human being and cultivating confidence in your abilities, intuition, and identity.

Despite all I've accomplished in my life, I have never particularly thought of myself as courageous or brave. I simply went out and *did* what I felt I wanted—and had—to do.

How Do We Be Brave?

The flip side of courage is fear. A lot of fear comes from having to make difficult decisions. Be prepared to make them and be prepared to sometimes fail. But don't think it's the end of the world if you do. In fact, it's a perfect opportunity to redo the decision or outcome and not be consumed by that failure. Whether it's inventions, people, civilizations, or history, we fixate on hundreds of grand successes but easily forget all the millions of mistakes that went into them along the way. We must never be afraid to take chances and seize opportunities to try something new. And don't ever remain so disappointed that it overrides your positive attitude.

How do we nurture and grow courage in ourselves? As I said before, fear is a primary barrier to courage. Find people whom you can trust and don't be afraid to talk about that fear with them. Whomever you choose, they must be people whose values you admire and whose advice resonates with you. Really make that effort to connect with them and not just with people your own age—different ages afford life perspectives that can be extremely valuable.

If you can't find a friend to talk to, how about finding someone you admire? Throughout my life, I've been inspired by some historical figures, like Abraham Lincoln, whose writing was incredible. A natural-born leader, he always knew he could be President of the United States, according to the biography *Team of Rivals* by Doris Kearns Goodwin. His courage, thoughtfulness, and deep insight into his own personality have always impressed me deeply, as well as his not being afraid to stand up for the common good and equality. I particularly love his intelligence, sensitivity, and his fabulous speeches.

Eleanor Roosevelt, the wife of another American president, Franklin D. Roosevelt, has also been a guiding force for me. Some of my favorite quotes are hers:

"No one can make you feel inferior without your consent."
"Courage is more exhilarating than fear and in the long run it is easier."
"It is easy to slip into self-absorption and it is equally fatal."

I believe that young people are particularly prone to fear. A natural part of adolescence is exploring identity, craving kinship with a peer group, and not wanting to stick out or be different from friends. But the frenetic scrutiny of social media has made this temptation to self-compare and conform so much worse. The online, anonymous nature of these platforms, which are deliberately designed to be compelling and addictive, allows one to freely criticize, bully, and troll without retribution or nuance. This intense, 24/7 assault is often emotionally devastating and can literally end lives; and it contributes to the overall social anxiety and depression now epidemic among teens and vulnerable young people.

How do we counteract this? One way is to remember that your fear about not knowing what to do or who to be is not unusual, so you're not that different from others after all. And it's okay to be different; you don't have to conform to every standard, every new trend, or every technological advancement. It's even okay not to be wearing it. Really.

And you just might be surprised at how people you don't know appreciate your differences.

It's also vitally important to seek out and be with people and organizations whose values you align with, preferably in person and not just online when possible. Remember that there's a difference between discussion and gossip; the latter is when you're talking about someone or something you're not necessarily familiar with. The perpetuation of rumors or subjects you don't really know anything about can lead to very serious, unintended effects.

Being Grateful

Courage means being grateful. Grateful for being alive, whether you're twenty-two or ninety-five. Grateful for being you, even if you don't think you have any talent or ability (you do, even if you don't see it yet). Grateful for the ability to set goals and hold hope.

Courage also means sometimes accepting the limitations of others—and doing it gracefully without a grudge. We all know people who are not living up to what we think of as their full potential. We get frustrated by seeing them make mistakes or sabotage themselves. However, it's not our duty to change them or dictate how they live their lives. We must remember that we can never fully understand one's situation or all the factors that affect how people have become who they are. The best we can do is to be supportive, not judgmental. Encouraging, not nagging. Positive, not negative.

Taking a Stand to Help Others

Courage is not being afraid to take a stand when you see people taking advantage of others less fortunate or unable to advocate for themselves. This was the impetus for me to start Silver Planet, a website that provided advice and tips for vulnerable elders who were getting phone calls from scammers asking for money. I've always felt emotionally drained and angry when I hear about someone taking advantage of the elderly and preying on their loneliness. I feel exactly the same way about people who don't treat others (especially those working in caregiving or service positions) with respect, decency, and fairness.

Being Brave in the Workplace

Courage is especially valuable when you stand up for yourself in the workplace, especially when you want a promotion. If you're a woman, you may have noticed that you're getting unequal pay compared to your male colleagues, or that you're not being offered the same career advancement opportunities. But figuring out how to broach these subjects can be tricky.

Sometimes we don't act because we're afraid of conflict, and our fear makes it hard to gather courage. But there is a difference between challenging and questioning. Challenging can trigger anger and defensiveness, especially when pride, ego, and reputation are on the line. But questioning, when it is done calmly, rationally, and logically, is far more powerful, especially when it's persistent and unwavering. It is assertion, not aggression. Remembering the difference can serve you well in life.

Let's take the workplace scenario in which you believe you're not being fairly compensated compared to a colleague. Much depends on the context: your history and length of time you've been with the company, your job performance, how long you've been in the position, and so on. Again, there is a difference between questioning and challenging. After all, you wouldn't just barge into your supervisor's office and complain, "Why am I getting paid twenty dollars less an hour than John?"

First, you must do your homework and research. Be prepared and equip yourself with accurate facts, not rumors or hearsay. Is the work you want truly available to you? Does your competence really compare to that of your colleague? You must be confident that you can do the job just as well and that you're equally qualified.

Second, be wise about your timing. Confronting your supervisor in front of others at a board meeting will not win you any favors. Instead, do it privately when they're in a good mood—and not right before lunch or a critical deadline.

Third, you need to be prepared to answer any questions the supervisor may ask, such as *How do you know this? What makes you think that you're at this level? Why is this an issue now?*

Next, how do you address differences of opinion without being demeaning? Remember that this is not the time to confront, no matter how angry or upset you might be. A conversation can't be started with confrontation. Keep your emotions under control and try to see the situation from the other person's perspective. Feel out if there is room for amicable, persuasive negotiation.

For instance, you can see if you can start a conversation around equal pay and equal time off. Remember, you're challenging an *issue*, not confronting the person. Offer to make your boss aware of different sides of that issue. Or open a supervisor's mind to an alternate perspective in a way that lets them come to conclusions on their own, so they think it was their idea.

If your supervisor is male and you're not, you may have a larger task at hand. The fact that he's a different gender means that he's very possibly operating under cultural and social prejudices that even he may not be fully aware of. Or perhaps his actions are deliberately intended to protect himself and his standing in the company (or others he aligns with). Don't be naive when you enter this situation, and never, ever play the part of the poor, disadvantaged woman. Instead, stay assertive, logical, and reasonable.

In these situations, never make the mistake of treating a supervisor the same as you would a coworker or a friend. In this case, they are not your buddy. Being professional, staying calm, remaining focused on the long game's end goal, and not taking things personally are all key.

Also, don't forget to be positive about your role: "Wouldn't you agree that I'm doing a comparable job with positive effects? I feel qualified, I'm prepared, and I want

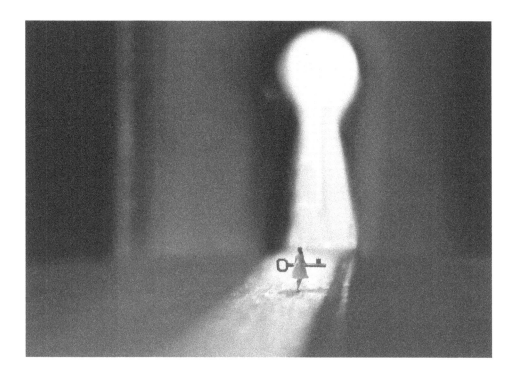

to continue to work with the company in a way that I can contribute even more."

If your supervisor says they'll take your request under consideration, hold them accountable timewise. Ask them if the matter can be taken up at the next board meeting. Do not wait or procrastinate in asking for results, but do not pester too soon either.

Once a decision is made, be prepared to respectfully listen to the supervisor's response. If your request is refused, you will need to have a plan for dealing with this and what those next steps might be. Don't challenge the decision unless you're prepared to carry through and to what extent and on what timeline. And while the outcome you want may not happen this time, stay alert for other opportunities and future timing.

Why do I speak about courage in the workplace? You might recall from the stockbroker chapter that I underwent this exact scenario when I worked for Robinson & Co. and wanted to move up to the coveted boardroom that was the sole domain of men.

I was careful never to bring up the fact that I was a woman not being treated equally. Instead, I reframed the issue by saying I wanted more opportunities to offer not just mutual funds but also other financial products. I knew there was no reason they could legitimately deny me because I'd already passed the exams to become a broker, plus I was a good producer for the company with a proven track record. You might recall that I first approached my immediate supervisor, Al Pitts, with a request for a transfer. I was very straightforward, direct, positive, and concise. I made sure to speak correctly, respectfully, and quietly, not emotionally or with any snarky tones. And I was not surprised by his negative response.

After Pitts declined me twice, I went directly to the boardroom supervisor. He too refused me for the same reason: "You're doing such a good job, why would you want to move?" I then decided to leave the matter alone for a month or two and not pester. When I calmly asked the boardroom supervisor again, he accepted me because the management knew by then that I'd simply quit, seek work at another company, and take my lucrative clients with me.

The key to all this was to be polite but assertive, patient but persistent, and prepared with facts and performance. I also didn't escalate the matter, become emotional, gossip, or complain to colleagues about it—any of these would have been grounds for confirming stereotyped perceptions of women somehow not being equal to their male counterparts. I was also keenly aware of timing.

Even today, it's all too easy for management to denigrate women as being too emotional and somehow not as capable of handling the pressure of holding executive positions in large corporations. As of January 2023, there are only fifty-three female CEOs of Fortune 500 companies, or just over 10 percent. The first female CEO of a major financial institution, Jane Fraser of Citibank, was appointed only in February 2021. I still hear the questioning tones in the voices of broadcast announcers and financial analysts when they discuss Fraser's work. That incredulity and doubt do not materialize when these same people discuss a new male being appointed to such a position. Instead, they say, *Let's give him a chance.*

Now, here's an opportunity for women to practice courage—and the rest of us to support them.

COURAGE IN PRISON

For several years, I volunteered every month with The Philly Project, a former nonprofit that focused on incarcerated populations. I cofounded it with another man with the same idea; our goal was to help prepare men for probation meetings with their supervisors. Later, when I lived in Colorado, I volunteered at a women's prison, where I taught courses in self-esteem and basic finance. I also visited inmates in one of the highest-security prisons in the entire country.

These experiences changed me profoundly. Few people understand what it's like to live in a prison or even who prisoners actually are. Volunteering in these facilities taught me not to judge people and to never make assumptions because one simply doesn't know what circumstances led to inmates being where they are. I learned not to be afraid to enter these places even when other people were horrified at the very thought of doing so. And I also had to resist becoming jaded by what I saw and heard behind these walls.

What did happen was that I witnessed the flaws of our American prison system on full display. It often spectacularly fails to provide adequate job opportunities or safe living or working conditions for the incarcerated. Many states have also discontinued the educational programs to help them get high school equivalencies, which are required to apply for the most basic jobs. And not enough is being done to help former inmates properly transition back to civilian living.

To survive inside a prison day after day takes far more courage, fortitude, and resilience than most of us can possibly imagine. Most prison inmates are not innately the bad people that society labels them. Many were born into abusive domestic situations where they were rejected, neglected, and made to feel inferior for just existing. Self-esteem is based on understanding, accepting, and liking yourself, and if no one models it for you or encourages you to feel good about your thoughts, beliefs, feelings, and desires, then how do you learn these life skills?

While some inmates I met did display deep cruelty and showed no remorse for their crimes, I realized that many people in prison had grown up in unfortunate circumstances from a young age, making the wrong choice in the wrong place at the wrong time. How might their stories have been different if someone had had the courage to intervene, validate their existence, and help them love and respect themselves? They would be living very different lives today. And they deserve second chances in society and in how we treat them.

Courage lives within and among us every day. You just need to call out its name and help others do the same.

6
REBUILDING HISTORY

Old City: Rehabilitated into New Life ~
Dreaming of Building and Building a Dream ~
Letitia Court ~ The Chocolate Factory ~
K/K Enterprises ~ The Castings ~ Reflections

I am an action visionary.
— Florence Klein —

f I had not become possibly the first female stockbroker in Philadelphia, had not
been a workaholic, had not been one of the few woman broker-dealers in the
United States in 1980, and had not gone on to develop major condominiums in
the City of Brotherly Love, what else would I have done?

I had never taken a class on architecture, nor did I have any background in or
any family who had ever been in the construction industry. I didn't even have any
contacts in the financial or banking world for real estate financing. Nor was I ever
a real estate agent—in fact, I never even liked that profession.

So, what gave me the vision and ideas to tackle development in the historic
Old City District in Philadelphia?

OLD CITY: REHABILITATED INTO NEW LIFE

I have always deeply appreciated the history of our country. I own an extensive
collection of books about Benjamin Franklin since he is one of my favorite historic
figures. I admire him for being a polymath and for his curiosity, courage, and remarkable ability to see a problem or a need and then find a solution. I'm also very
fond of President Abraham Lincoln because of his distinctly humane personality,
skillful oratory, and eloquent writing.

Philadelphia founder William Penn named the city after a Greek word for
brotherly love. In 1682, before the Revolutionary War, Penn appointed the sur-
veyor Thomas Holmes to lay out the original city in five squares so that Penn could
market it as a "greene country towne" along the Delaware River. Incorporating
Penn's ideas into urban planning, Holmes drew up the city in an orderly grid

pattern to allow for easy travel, provide residential areas with open green spaces, and prevent the spread of fire (a huge hazard in those days).

By 1683, most of the east and west streets had been laid out, many named after varieties of trees. One area would become Old City, about twenty-five square blocks destined to become the original commercial center of Philadelphia, bound by the Delaware River on the east, Fifth Street on the west, Chestnut Street on the south, and Vine Street on the north. This is where Philadelphia as we know it first started and where tradesmen came to establish businesses, setting up shops and naming them after the products they manufactured and sold. (For instance, the Castings, which started in 1697, specialized in sewer covers and fittings.)

As you might imagine, this was always a bustling place, a central district for brisk commerce and vigorous intellectual activity following British and Quaker colonialist settlement. A teenage Benjamin Franklin arrived here from Boston in 1723 and walked up Market Street, then known as High Street. Young Ben found a job as a printer's apprentice, later set up his own printing shop, and the rest is history. Ultimately, the key historic figures who crafted our Declaration of Independence and the Constitution would regularly gather at the nearby City Tavern on Second Street to debate political ideas or attend religious services at the nearby Christ Church—thus shaping the thinking that would give birth to American democracy and independence.

Old City remains a truly vibrant, thriving place, saturated in immense history. Independence Hall, its surrounding national park, Elfreth's Alley, Carpenters' Hall, and the Betsy Ross House are all here within easy walking distance, complete with actors dressed in Colonial-style clothing on some occasions. Visitors can view Ben Franklin's grave, where pennies are still thrown for good luck, or attend the same historic Christ Church as America's forefathers did—it continues to hold religious services more than three centuries later.

DREAMING OF BUILDING AND BUILDING A DREAM

In 1979, I was living in my suburban home in the community of Dresher, which is in the Montgomery Township about ten miles north of Philadelphia. Dresher lies between an older community called Flourtown on the west and Glenside on the east.

If I did not drive in to work on the beautiful, twisting Lincoln Drive, I usually caught a commuter train so I could arrive at work by eight in the morning. By then, I was in my forties, my children were all out of the house and in college, and I decided I wanted to live closer to my office in Philly's central business district, Center City, which encompasses both modern skyscrapers and historical Old City, the birthplace of American independence.

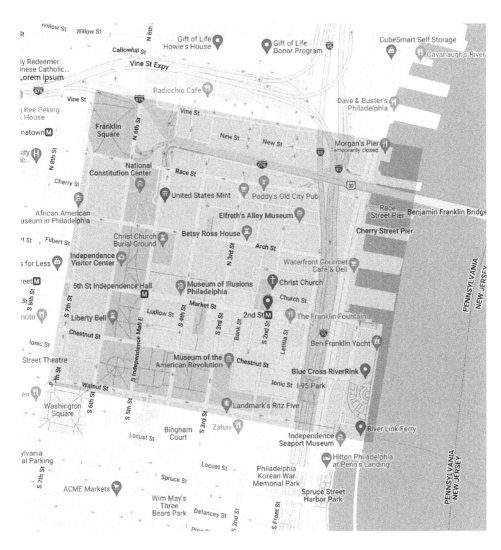

A map of Old City in Philadelphia (in the shaded gray area). It spans north to south from Vine Street to Walnut Street, and west to east from Seventh Street to the Delaware River.

But when I started to look for a suitable home here, it turned out that I was not alone. This was a time when many other suburbanites were interested in moving from their large, empty-nest places into the historic homes of Society Hill and Old City. Here, the fact that new restaurants with exciting menus seemed to be opening every week, live theatre and try-outs for Broadway shows were flourishing, and renowned art museums rubbed shoulders with numerous cultural institutions nearby made this area a very appealing place to live—and still at very affordable prices.

Yet I could not find a living space to buy and own that I liked. Most residences were apartments in large old buildings that had not yet been converted to condominiums. Any available historic houses were often extremely narrow, with small, dark rooms that reflected the architectural style of when they were built but not the less formal, more casual lifestyles of today. I craved open space, plenty of natural light, and airy beauty. Instead of settling for one of these dimly lit, claustrophobic places, I simply decided to seek a property that I could renovate myself in Old City. As you might imagine, it didn't take me long to start investigating what buildings might be for sale.

It was a real joy to walk on the uneven pavement of Old City's cobblestone streets despite the four-inch heels that I sometimes wore when coming straight from work. I felt as though I were literally walking in the footsteps of our country's founders nearly several hundred years ago. I trod through narrow alleys and peeked into darkened, stained windows of former factories and warehouses. These huge, mostly brick structures deeply intrigued me, and I began to envision what they could become. I saw Old City as an opportunity to convert these deserted industrial buildings and make them alive again for the current generation.

The famous Elfreth's Alley in Old City, the oldest continuously inhabited street in the United States.

By the 1970s, Old City had been neglected for years, and it was showing. Artists occupied some of its decrepit buildings, attracted by cheap rent and abundant natural light. The zoning code was changed from industrial to commercial in 1971, but the city's planning commission found that more than half of this district's buildings were in poor condition, vandalized, and vacant.

The surviving businesses that still occupied the remaining buildings had often been there for decades. Typically, they were small wholesale jobbers that serviced retail stores throughout Philadelphia, specializing in a particular line of products. For instance, those on Front and Second Streets sold only men's socks, underwear, work pants, and shirts. Some were still identified by their functions—the Hoop-skirt Factory or the Box Shop. Samuel's, for instance, on North Third Street, sold economically priced everyday house dresses, dusters, and aprons for women who would come down in streetcars, make their purchases, and hurry home before their children finished school for the day. Looking at these venerable buildings that had seen so much change on both sides of their walls over the decades inspired a deep desire within me to preserve them and give them another chance.

By the time I came on the scene, some of these buildings were already being renovated into apartment complexes. Soon they'd be occupied by young office workers, former suburbanites, and empty nesters like me who all wanted a taste of the excitement being generated around this historic area in the 1970s and 1980s. As the *Philadelphia Inquirer* reported on October 9, 1983, "The physical transformation alone has been astounding. In twenty years, the street has gone from a crowded, dirty, down-at-the heels marketplace to a vibrant retail center and transportation hub … the area was terribly blighted … and in another ten to twenty years it will achieve a place of greatness."

Given my lack of background in real estate, what obstacles did I encounter as I explored Old City's brick-paved streets? Initially, not that many, surprisingly. I joined the Old City Civic Association, introduced myself to its president Bill Kingsley and others, and became a regular at their Thursday early-morning meetings. Most of the people on this committee were men with businesses in the area or diligent, concerned citizens who wanted to keep the neighborhood's historic flavor alive. New developers had to submit their building plans to the Old City development committee, and details such as parking, building height, and general size had to receive its approval. Aside from the committee, the city also required that any new buildings or renovations must aesthetically fit in with this historic area.

The Hoopskirt Factory Lofts at 309 to 313 Arch Street in Old City. Originally a petticoat factory, the building was constructed in 1875, renovated into apartments by my good friend and architect David Beck in 1980, and converted into condos in 2006.

In beginning my search, I'd follow a lead from the committee and then wander into a store that might be full of old lighting fixtures or wholesale dry goods. These businesses had typically been in the area for many years or even decades, and their proprietors were delighted to start a conversation with a smiling "young" face. Once they learned the reason for my interest, our talks would uncover bittersweet thoughts about their retirement, legacy, and how their past—as well as those of the buildings they occupied—might evolve into a hopeful future.

After I located and renovated one building that I lived in myself (the Chocolate Factory), I became hooked! I soon found others and negotiated several purchases. Once I made a "handshake" deal with the owner of the aforementioned Hoopskirt

Factory. My process was to always negotiate the price and the terms, shake hands on it, and then return with the funding. Back then, I earnestly believed that once you shook hands, you had a firm deal.

Well, the Hoopskirt owner did not believe in the same standard. When I went back to see him the very next day, he declared, "Oh, I just sold this building to a New York man."

"What?" I exclaimed, stunned. "You made a deal with me for $250,000! We shook hands!"

The expression on his face pushed me aside with a look that smacked of "You're just a woman." Ironically, the NYC buyer never came through and the Hoopskirt man ended up not selling his building for several years. In the meantime, undaunted, I moved on to other buildings. Surprisingly, I never encountered gender discrimination after the Hoopskirt owner, probably because I was already known in the finance world in Philadelphia and had a proven track record.

Letitia Court

In 1977, Len and I, along with several others, found a suitable building in Old City to purchase and develop. Built in 1890, it was all brick, stood five stories tall, and had an adjacent parking lot. It was also very conveniently located and attractively priced. Since the entire area was designated as historic, the city of Philadelphia and the federal government were allowing substantial tax incentives to renovate these old, dilapidated structures. This one faced Front Street on the Delaware River in the area known as Penn's Landing (the original landmark name for Old City).

A 2,100-square-foot Italian restaurant was already renting the building's first floor. Our architect drew up plans to accommodate fourteen residential units, which included eleven one-bedroom apartments and three studio apartments, all light-filled from large windows that faced the water, the courtyard, or the rear street, Letitia. Hence, we named the building Letitia Court—after the street made famous by the many times it was mentioned in Benjamin Franklin's writings—and named for William Penn's daughter.

Although we had several partners in this venture, I was in charge and no one else contributed much except funds. It was my first time working with an architect, but the timing felt right. But, before we could start construction, we received an offer from Stephen Solms, a young Philadelphia developer who was interested in purchasing our interest in the project. Since the market seemed to be changing and we knew Steve would be a good steward of the property, we accepted his offer, and I had no regrets about the sale. Today, these units are rental apartments that are usually fully occupied, as this is still a prime location in Old City.

THE CHOCOLATE FACTORY

Since I still wanted to live in Center City, I continued to scour various areas, including Old City, Northern Liberties, and Rittenhouse Square, which were all short walks to my office. Len and I heard that an empty four-story brick building, nearly a century old and once a chocolate factory, was for sale. Bordered by Front and Second Streets on the east-west and Market Street (originally called High Street) and Arch Street on the south-north, it was a fabulous location in the heart of our nation's history. Len and I purchased the building for $145,000 from an architect who was reluctant to sell it. But he was convinced when I told him that our plans were not to destroy the essence of the building but to retain its unique character and not turn it into tiny spaces—a vision that he and I already had in common.

I was so very excited!

Our building had been the home of Marquetand's Candy Company, which made specialty chocolates. Philadelphia was, in fact, once the center of many chocolate manufacturers; Whitman's (of the Sampler fame) began in 1842 at Third and Market Streets, just half a block from the Chocolate Factory, and both Reese's Peanut Butter Cups and the original Hershey Kisses also originated in Philly.

The first time Len and I entered the Chocolate Factory, we discovered large, dusty, double-sided oak desks still sitting on the second floor. We also found tables covered with mirrors on which chocolates were once sorted by hand to cull out the ones whose color had changed while the individual pieces tempered.

(As an aside: After I moved into the Chocolate Factory to my own apartment, I received a postcard from a woman in Arizona addressed to the Marquetand's Candy Company requesting if they would send her a box of buttercreams. A woman never forgets her chocolates, and the firm was known for this specialty. Now Amazon sells Philadelphia buttercreams made in assorted delicious flavors with luscious melt-in-your-mouth centers. I think I'll order a box today.)

It turned out to be very difficult to find financing for the Chocolate Factory, much more than I'd expected. Mortgage interest rates had risen substantially, and banks were not willing to work with unknown developers without deep pockets.

Especially unwelcome was my idea to make it into eight loft condominium units. Although they're very common now in urban areas, this type of condo was most unusual for the time, and Philly was slow to catch on to loft residences despite their popularity in New York starting in the late 1970s. In fact, they became all the rage in trendy SoHo, with one *New York Times* article from February 1977 declaring this headline: "Conversions of Commercial Buildings Offering Novelty to Tenants." The article declared the SoHo loft buildings as "spiritual fathers of the movement," and it quoted developer Sam Brody saying that "because of the idiosyncrasies, the accidents of these old buildings—they suggest all kinds of ways to break out from standard apartments."

So, I decided to advertise our condominiums as "A Little Bit of SoHo in Old City." But the concept of open-loft condo design was so new to Philadelphia that I had trouble convincing our lenders that the units were a viable business prospect. And because this was a historic area, obtaining the necessary building permits was a much more stringent process. All this, on top of the usual building delays, caused many anxious meetings and difficulties. I always envision things about ten years ahead, and Philly is typically slow to catch on to innovation. Certainly, its banks are notoriously hesitant and conservative, even today in 2023.

Nonetheless, I managed to move forward and arrange the necessary financing. Our plan had been to initially sell the units as condos, but since we also needed to stay afloat and cover our loans, we began renting them out until we could eventually find buyers for all the units. Rent started at $750 a month for a 1,250-square-foot unit and went up to $1,350 for a 2,450-square-foot unit.

In 1982, a local weekly newspaper declared,

The Chocolate Factory, south of Market Street, east of 2nd Street. **Plus:** If you can find it, you really deserve a box of chocolates. **Minus:** Great textbook example of what can happen when a successful stock-broker tries to become a successful developer of loft apartments in a

city that never had a demand for lofts, especially for lofts with six-figure price tags. Flo Klein is moving in herself from her seashore pad, but she doesn't really need all seven condos, so stop by and haggle."

Once the funding was finally in place, we hired David Beck, an architect who had studied with the legendary, award-winning University of Pennsylvania architect Louis Kahn. Considered one of the greatest twentieth-century American architects, Kahn was known for combining Modernism with the weight and dignity of ancient monuments, and his respect for a sense of place and his remarkable creative vision made David just the perfect architect to redesign the Chocolate Factory. In a *New York Times* article published on December 18, 1984, David was quoted: "An alley is just wide enough for trees and narrow enough to keep people together. It feels safe, it feels warm, and everybody knows everybody."

I should mention something here about the alleys in Philadelphia's Old City. These are not the usual dirty, somewhat menacing alleys of a modern big city, but an intimate world of incredibly narrow streets densely lined with picturesque brick homes, complete with wide shutters and distinctive, slanted basement-entry doors that take you back several hundred years to when they were built. Mascher and Cuthbert Streets are both what you'd call alleys, the former built with blue cobblestones that date

The Chocolate Factory is one of those special projects, the kind that are multiplying in Old City. Many cities have a treasure trove of vacant warehouses and mills, which for many years were seen as white elephants.

But through a number of incentives — historic preservation and tax write-offs or shelters for developers — and the willingness of lenders to back architectural plans for

Please see **FACTORY** Page **E2**

Architect David Beck with Florence Klein at the Chocolate Factory.

Bulletin Photos by Frederick A. Meyer

The Chocolate Project was featured in a newspaper article about the changing rejuvenation of old factories and warehouses in Old City. I'm pictured with architect David Beck above.

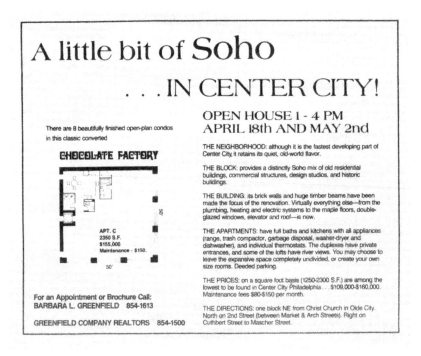

to the early eighteenth century, when they were taken from the Delaware and Schuylkill Rivers. Each two-to-seven-inch-long stone was washed, cleaned, and hand-assembled to line these alleys. The oldest continuously inhabited street in America, Elfreth's Alley, is also lined with these cobblestones and sits just one block north of the Chocolate Factory.

With his keen awareness and appreciation for these extraordinary surroundings, David ultimately came up with a marvelous design for our eight loft condominiums, including a penthouse unit on the top floor with a residence for Len and me. The four units in the original building measured twenty-five by twenty-five feet and were connected by an elevator to a new section, which was built on the empty lot next to the original building. This new building contained an additional four units of about 1,300 square feet each.

Because the Chocolate Factory building came with an existing elevator core, and an adjoining empty lot offered parking on the ground level, we built a new lobby where you entered the elevator. The elevator then opened directly into the individual units, like in New York, which made for surprising, stunning entrances—huge, open rooms with beautiful exposed-brick walls, handsome hemlock ceilings about eighteen feet high, and four stout oak posts in the center of each maple floor. And how I've wished many times that I could have kept those original gorgeous Marquetand's desks—not much furniture of that size, quality, and durability is made anymore!

Architect David Beck's sketches of the loft condominiums of the Chocolate Factory. The elevator opened directly into the individual units, like in New York. The lofts featured huge, open rooms with beautiful exposed-brick walls, eighteen-foot-high hemlock ceilings, and stout oak posts in the center of each maple floor, with plenty of natural light flooding in through the existing factory windows. Although these design features are common now in urban residences in converted buildings, this kind of open plan was revolutionary in the 1980s, and it caused a sensation in conservative, traditional Philadelphia.

Len and I in our own penthouse condo in the Chocolate Factory. I adored the huge, open living room.

Since the historic neighborhood of Old City was heavily governed by building codes, one had to be extremely aware of what renovations could be done—and not. And if you were seeking tax write-offs, you had to be even more careful.

According to the tax-credit incentives for renovation in 1983 when I was working on these properties, a developer could receive up to 25 percent credit for a nationally registered historic landmark, 20 percent for a forty-year-old building without such august status, and 15 percent for a building thirty years or older. These credits were taken the first year a building was placed in use. In addition, owners of properties renovated after 1981 could write off their costs in fifteen years, compared with the previous depreciation period of fifty years. This meant that the potential after-tax rate of return on investment could be far greater than that of conventional profits, and standard accounting practices allowed these credits.

When we developed the Chocolate Factory in the early 1980s, we had hoped to get some of these write-offs. But it's a tricky business. We made a change to the windows that did not exactly conform to the building's original windows, so although the building remained a part of the historic area, we were disqualified from getting the write-off. Years later, one of the condo owners wanted to raise the roof to allow additional room to enter the roof from the top floor, but the city's historic planning division would not authorize this extension.

CONTEMPORARY		
SECOND FLOOR	$750.00	1250 s/f
THIRD FLOOR	$775.00	1250 s/f
FOURTH FLOOR	$850.00	1250 s/f
CHOCOLATE BUILDING		
SECOND FLOOR	$1200.00	2350 s/f
THIRD FLOOR	$1250.00	2350 s/f
Bi-LEVEL-MASCHER	$1200.00	2150 s/f
Bi-LEVEL-CUTHBERT	$1350.00	2450 s/f

A realty flyer advertising the units in the Chocolate Factory. We'd planned to initially sell the units as condos, but since we also needed to generate income to cover our loans, we rented them out until we could eventually find buyers for all the units. Rent started at $750 a month for a 1,250-square-foot unit and went up to $1,350 for a 2,450-square-foot unit. Today, these condos are valued between $600,000 to more than $1,000,000.

After three years of planning, delays, and exhausting renovation, our building was finally ready. In the spring of 1982, my dear sister-in-law Sharon took a day off from work to help us move into our place—a very long day and evening! David's design for our penthouse was an open concept with a spacious feeling, enhanced by high large windows that opened directly onto the roof. Our loft was simply wonderful, the site of so many wonderful gatherings and parties; I enjoyed hosting holiday dinners here with our growing family. I remember my grandson Nathaniel sitting at the piano when he was three years old, my holding a party for my brother's twentieth wedding anniversary, and the look of surprise when my dear friend Marsha walked in with her daughter on her sixty-fifth birthday.

For my fiftieth birthday, I threw an Alice in Wonderland party. Paraphrasing the words of Lewis Carroll on an invitation, I requested that everyone bring a teacup and wear a hat for admission. I divided the sixty guests into two groups. After drinking champagne out of the teacups, the guests were directed down the rabbit hole (our closed fire escape) and out into Old City in two groups. One group was to meet the Queen of Hearts (this was my daughter Kim) on the corner of Arch and Second streets, while the other group met Tweedledum and Tweedledee (Len's mother and her second husband) sitting on a bench by Christ Church.

Our friends made several more such stops to end up at a local Old City restaurant, where I met them afterward. As I was opening gifts, would you believe that I fell sound asleep—too tired after a drink of gin—and missed the rest of the evening. Nothing like going out like a light—what a party!

Despite the immense renovation and construction difficulties, I never had a second thought about the Chocolate Factory project. In the end, the individual eight condo units became seven when one owner combined two apartments on the same level to form a single spectacular living space of nearly 3,800 square feet. It is selling for well over a million dollars now. How times have changed.

Everyone loves these condos, and since there are only seven of them, they are truly unique. Their owners are committed to cherishing them, and they have bonded as a community and usually hold a street party every year for the Memorial Day or Fourth of July holiday.

I continued to live in the Chocolate Factory until 1999, even after my 1986 divorce from Len after thirty-two years of marriage. I sold the last of the units in October 2019; I still love that building and regret that I ever sold my residence. They're still the most beautiful condo homes to live in.

K/K Enterprises

In 1986, I was directed to a property owned by Harry Caplan, one of many he had in Old City. He was a well-known figure in town, dubbed "the mayor of Second

Street" from a rumor that at one time he had purchased all the buildings on the long block of Second that ran from Arch to Race Streets. As a small child, he had played on the banks of the Delaware River, throwing stones into its waters. Harry often told me how he had sold packages of toothpicks on the corner of High Street (now called Market).

I first met Harry at his business, the famous National Store. I found him to be a very brusque man, about seventy years old with a no-time-for-small-talk attitude. This was the first building I ever negotiated with Harry, except that I'm not certain if there was actual negotiation. If you wanted to purchase a building from Harry Caplan, he set the price; if you accepted it, then that was it. A mere $750,000 and this property was mine. It included a large parking lot and two old, completely uninhabitable, derelict buildings on 208 Arch Street across from the Betsy Ross House. I named that property K/K Enterprises.

Because both buildings were designated as having historic status, they could not be torn down. For a few years, I ran the parking lot as a separate business and then developed a plan to have it and the buildings converted into a Hampton Hotel, as the area badly needed lodging facilities. In a report, the Old City Civic Association stated this:

> [There is] much to like about the project … the concept of a hotel usage here won very favorable positive approval. Your sensitivity to the neighborhood's longstanding concern with liquor licenses and restaurants served your project well … in the area of design, the committee was very pleased by the obvious intention to make the building fit in with the historic surroundings.

We secured a franchise for this Hampton as well as a unique bond issue that I negotiated with the city of Philadelphia (the first of its kind), plus an Urban Development Action grant. Unfortunately, interest rates then shot up to 16 percent, and not enough funds were available to begin the hotel's development. After countless lawyers, delays, and sleepless nights, I ended up selling the site and its buildings in 2004.

In November 2016, new developers discovered a most unusual find as they dug the foundation for a ten-story, 116-unit apartment complex with two underground parking levels at 281 Arch Street—more than four hundred skeletons of children and adults and nearly eighty coffins dating to the 1700s. According to an article from the local CBS affiliate on March 9, 2017:

> The coffins were part of the First Baptist Church Burial Ground established in 1707, when Benjamin Franklin was just a year old.

125 New Jobs

Office and Retail Complex To Be Built

BY KENT REICHERT

A new office and retail complex soon to be built in Old City could bring 125 new jobs to the area in the next year.

The project, at 218-230 Arch St., will include a 40,000 square foot, four story complex of office space as well as 4,000 square feet of retail shopping space and a 200-car garage, according to its developer, Florence Klein.

The new jobs that are expected to be created include 100 office positions, 10 retail positions and 15 parking lot attendant positions, according to figures provided by the Philadelphia Industrial Development Corporation (PIDC).

Construction will begin next Spring and be completed by Spring 1988.

The project will be developed through Klein's K/K Enterprises and designed by the Philadelphia firm Alesker, Reiff & Dundon Architects.

According to Klein, the project will be funded, in part, by an $825,000 federal Urban Development Action Grant (UDAG) which K/K Enterprises received in September.

The project is expected to cost $6,271,000 according to Ellen Brown, a UDAG project manager with the PIDC, which is the federal government's agent in Philadelphia for UDAG applications.

According to Klein, two historically certified buildings on the site will be preserved.

"We had permission to tear down the buildings," if renovating them would have proved unfeasible.

But after discussing various possibilities with the architects and the historian for the City of Philadelphia, Richard Tyler, Klein decided that it was possible to save the buildings.

"We plan to keep the buildings and incorporate them into the facade of the new project," Klein said.

Tyler told the *South Street Star* that the buildings are four-story, loft-type structures, built in the mid 19th-century.

Tyler said that while the two structures had no extraordinary historical significance by themselves, they help to maintain the architectural fabric of the area.

"It is a case where the whole is greater than the sum of the parts," said Tyler.

Florence Klein stands in front of Classic Courts, 232 N. 3rd St., one of several projects she is developing in Old City.

PHOTO BY A. GREGORIO McDONALD

Old City Civic Association president, Bill Kingsley, said he welcomed the project. "It will mean getting 200 cars off the street, which is encouraging. Also, the commercial space it will bring is important to us. We made a commitment long ago to maintain a mix of residential and commercial space in Old City" to keep the community vital.

Klein is currently also the developer of Classic Courts, 232 N. 3rd St. The 19-unit apartment building will be completed by the end of the year.

Another Klein project, the Castings Building, Bread and Quarry streets, will also be completed by the end of this month. ★

A newspaper article about K/K Enterprises. This was during the height of my time as a real estate developer in Philadelphia; I was also working on Classic Courts and the Castings at the same time.

Records show the bodies should have been moved to the Mount Moriah Cemetery in Southwest Philadelphia around 1860, but historians agree that someone didn't do their job.

"It's a business unfortunately and sometimes it's cheaper to cut corners in a business," Dr. Lee Arnold with the Historical Society of Pennsylvania told Eyewitness News.

…

The coffins were far below the standard six feet we know today, but that doesn't mean they were buried deep. Layers of streets have been added over time.

"They wouldn't have had to dig the bodies this low, six feet under was plenty. In winter it was almost impossible to bury somebody," Philadelphia historian Ed Mauger told Eyewitness News.

Lenny Ryan works across the street from the construction site and says given Philadelphia's history, the discovery is not surprising. "I'm sure if they excavated a lot of this city, they'd find a lot more," Ryan said.

My Old City made it in the news again!

THE CASTINGS

My next purchase from Harry Caplan, who was now my friend, was a set of old buildings on North Bread Street around the corner from the Betsy Ross House. Harry had decided that he wanted to tear the main building down so he could build a large new apartment complex. Since this was in a historic section with regulations that prohibited such demolition, Harry thought if he backed a large tractor carrying heavy equipment against this building's walls, its historic façade would be so damaged that he'd be allowed to just bring the rest of it down. Its outer brick wall was already crumbling from age, and rumors began floating in the neighborhood as to just what Harry Caplan was planning.

This property was not a usual lot with one primary building, but an entire complex that covered nearly an entire city block, with an adjacent small piece of empty land on North Bread Street. My vision was to create an entire apartment village within the complex, with studio and one- and two-bedroom lofts built within the older buildings, and to connect them with two new structures and incorporated enclosed courtyards. A soaring four-story lobby that was part of one of the original buildings was filled with natural light, mezzanine walkways, and two huge enclosed areas. One of our goals was to preserve and display as many of the original artifacts found on the property as possible, which had housed a metal-casting foundry that operated for more than two hundred years.

This fusion of old and new on such an ambitious scale set the Castings apart from most historic renovations of the time. In those days, most such designs were implemented within only one old building, typically a large warehouse. But ours was meant to aesthetically integrate both modern structures with the site's older buildings in a most striking, inviting way of urban life while fully respecting its storied past.

The property had originally been owned by Joseph Oat and Sons, a metal-casting foundry that started in 1787 and went out of business in 1983. During its nearly two centuries, the company created a remarkable array of industrial-use metal products, from copper tanks, condensing coils, and vacuum stills to cooling tanks, solvent recovery apparatuses, and heat exchangers. Orders came in from across the country and the world for these pieces of equipment, large and small, that were used in the production of countless chemicals, foods, and finished goods.

Before our construction began, I thoroughly investigated the four original buildings myself. Walking up creaky, unreliable stairs in my high heels right after coming from my office, I was soon covered with cobwebs, dust, wood, and other bits of age. But I found countless delightful surprises, such as beautiful chestnut and walnut shapes that turned out to be wooden sewer covers, as well as various tools and closures made by this large, very reliable firm. I collected many of these artifacts, converted their distinctive shapes into large wooden frames for mirrors, and sold them at the Sunday morning flea market, where I was always joined by my amazingly talented sister-in-law Sharon, who created her own lovely handmade brooches and bracelets. We still laugh at the time when the wind blew the pieces off our tables.

I discovered other treasures as well. Left behind were numerous product order invoices and requests from well-known companies for specific parts, often on beau-tifully illustrated letterhead stationery, as was the custom of the day. (Remember, there was no email, barely telephones, and not even planes to whisk paper mail—or manufactured parts—to their destination within hours—just regular mail, trains, and boats that often took many days or even weeks to arrive.)

These fascinating orders included one dated 1919 from the Breyer Ice Cream Co. (which still makes delicious flavors!), a 1914 specimen from Rub-No-More Co., which made washing powder and the famous Carbo-Naptho soap, and a 1918 letter from Mint Products Co., maker of Life Savers—yep, as in those round white mint candies with the hole in the middle. And here's a shocking find: A request for a copper pipe from the Pennsylvania State Lunatic Hospital in 1906. There were also beautifully stamped envelopes sent from places as far away as China, Russia, and Italy, inquiring about the availability of this or that.

Reading these original papers and surrounded by gigantic brick and stone walls that had borne witness to two centuries of bustle, workers, and changes, I was transported back in time. I also keenly felt the gravity and solemn responsibility of taking this once-world-renowned place into its next stage of history, and I wanted to do it justice.

THE CASTINGS

THE COMPLEX

The Castings is a unique apartment village. Occupying almost
an entire city block, these bril-
liantly adapted buildings achieve
an ideal balance between individual privacy and the vibrancy of
center city living.

Fine wood trusses accent the
former crane bay, now a light-
filled 4-story lobby featuring a
mezzanine walkway and a permanent display of museum-quality
industrial artifacts discovered
during renovation.

Two airy interior courtyards for
residents only offer an inviting
atmosphere of trees, plantings,
and seating areas.

Exciting modern amenities
include a comprehensive security
system, ultra-silent elevator,
separate, lockable storage areas,
a bicycle room, and a mail room.

The Castings. For those who
seek a uniquely enhanced quality
of urban life.

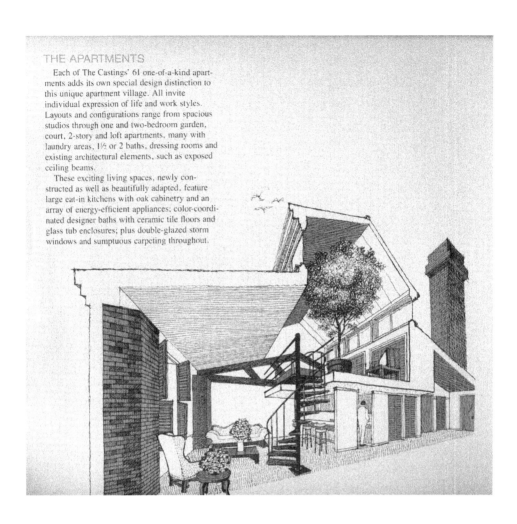

I was very excited to get David Beck again as the architect. Besides his work on the Chocolate Factory, he'd been involved in many of the city's other historic building conversions, bringing order out of chaos. Having learned the hard way from my mistakes with the Chocolate Factory, I made sure to structure the Castings project very carefully.

Since the tax incentives and standards of historically certified buildings meant we had to conduct our renovation of the Castings with extreme care, we meticulously analyzed every structural aspect of our buildings, down to the minutest details. One day, while excavating for a foundation, we were shocked to discover a very deep section with tile floors about three floors below grade. Surprise! Of course, the city's historic commission had us halt all construction until their federal and local historic building officials could examine it.

The Philadelphia Inquirer / JOHN COSTELLO

Klein walks past some of the machinery used when foundry was operating in Castings complex

While the origin of this section was never definitively determined, we believed it was a type of saloon, like the kind you might see in spaghetti westerns (it was really just a bar). It might have even possibly been a passageway from the Underground Railroad since we were just two blocks from the Delaware River. We were required to install a set of stairs from the building's lobby that descended into the space, complete with a door to be opened only by a special lock. We also had to provide an access route to the area, even though no one who lives in the building is even aware of this entrance. Rules, rules, rules!

Thanks to David's incredible designs and our careful attention to preserving these buildings, the Castings was awarded a National Register of Historic Places in the early 1990s, commemorated by a metal sign attached to the front door of the main entrance of the buildings. This made an unimaginable difference in the prestige of the property. And this status meant we would be eligible for those requisite tax credits—for that we were utterly ecstatic and relieved. What a spectacular celebration we held when the buildings were finally completed in 1989!

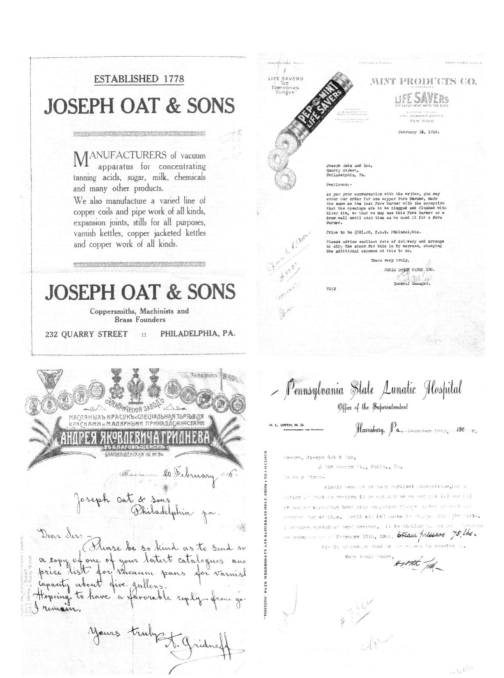

A few of the many Joseph Oat & Sons product orders, invoices, and brochures we found in the Castings building before we started to renovate. These were breathtaking in their variety, the quality of the stationery used, and the number of far-flung countries requesting parts and catalogs.

But tax laws were changing quickly, and it was critical to get all the units sold before the end of the 1986 tax year. I marketed the building as containing a minimum of five apartment units to qualified investors, each of whom needed to show at least one million dollars in assets.

I was quoted in the *Philadelphia Inquirer* on March 9, 1986:

> "When you looked at the complex from the outside, it didn't look like anything," said Florence Klein, president of American Classic. "In fact, it was once slated for demolition, but there was a big noise about it by the Philadelphia Historic Preservation Corp. and that was denied....
>
> "There were just empty crane buildings, no floors at all," said Klein. "But each of the buildings had its own integral layout, and he [Beck] did a tremendous job. There will be no long, narrow halls, and all the apartments will have tremendous light. Special efforts were made to maintain large windows and other unusual design features."
>
> The lobby of the complex will open on Bread Street, and its ceiling will be four stories up. A large overhead crane used in the foundry work will be left in place in the lobby, as will some catwalks formerly used by workers. [The catwalks were turned into hallways, and on the left side of the hallway were true loft apartments facing the high windows onto Cherry Street.] Also left will be exposed beams and other architectural features of the original building.
>
> Two open areas inside the complex will be landscaped and converted to courtyards. Several pieces of foundry equipment [found in an upper area of the original building], including an old vise table [from one of the back rooms] that will become a picnic table, will be blended into the courtyard decorations.

The Castings had forty-four one-bedroom apartments that were originally rented for $600 a month in the 1960s; in 2022, they sometimes rented for more than $1,200. The building also included ten two-bedroom and eight studio units for a total of sixty-two residences. The Castings has since been converted into desirable condos.

REFLECTIONS

I must say that writing this chapter has brought back such wonderful memories of working on these buildings. When I lived in Old City, the cobblestone streets that I saw daily outside my windows constantly reminded me of the historic figures who walked them long before—Benjamin Franklin, James Madison, and other creators of the Constitution.

Despite my success in real estate, it was never my intention to become the "woman developer" of Old City, Philadelphia. I simply wanted to find a home in

Center City within walking distance from my office on Market Street. It was only after I tasted the intricacies of developing eight loft condominiums in the Chocolate Factory that I became so inspired to search for other dingy, derelict century-old buildings that I could turn into light-filled, exciting modern living spaces.

It has now been nearly forty-five years since I worked on Letitia Court, the Chocolate Factory, the Castings, and another project called Classic Court. Much has happened since. These buildings have continued to be among the most popular residential renovations in Philadelphia, and the pure joy I feel in writing about them now is still the same thrilling happiness I experienced back then in seeing these buildings take new life, preserving them for others to enjoy, contributing to Philadelphia's history, and keeping it alive for current and future generations.

Today, in 2022, Old City's residents are a diverse, lively blend of working professionals, empty nesters, single older people, young folks starting families, and retired suburbanites who no longer want to mow lawns but simply enjoy the marvelous dining and art scene in this very walkable part of Philadelphia.

As I've related, it is not simple to renovate old buildings into modern living spaces. You need great architects, stable financing, good builders, competent union crews (Philadelphia is a union city through and through), outstanding supervisors on the job, excellent management, and careful attention to every single legal and building detail. But, as I found with my Old City projects—each one needing immense individual attention—the results can be stunning and incredibly rewarding. They truly brought out the creativity and leadership skills in me, as well as in the countless dedicated others who were part of my teams.

A resident of a condo in the Castings once wrote me this note:

> My building still looks like the factory it was for about 150 years. In fact, people trying to find it often pass it by. When they enter the high atrium with its factory artifacts now on the walls, they're always awed by its uniqueness. It isn't a cookie-cutter apartment building, and it doesn't have a bunch of frills that you have to pay for.

> —Carol

7
VOLUNTEERING

The Young Adult Group ~ Anne Frank House ~
AIDS Information Network ~ Center for Prevention of Domestic Violence ~
Hadassah ~ Women's Prisons in Colorado ~ USP Florence ADMAX

Helping the world is necessary to me.
— Florence Klein —

Throughout my life, I have always volunteered with organizations one way or another. Volunteering is in my DNA. No matter what stage of life I was in—as a mother, stockbroker, investment professional, real estate developer, or founder of Silver Planet—I always felt it was necessary to help others. It's just part of who I am. I began serving in my thirties and always worked with nonprofits.

Over the decades, I've joined various organizations, but if I felt my presence was truly not making a difference within a reasonable time, I didn't linger just to attend another meeting, take up space, or feed my ego. But if I could make concrete change for a certain cause or an overlooked demographic, whether it was prison inmates, Jewish women, developmentally disabled teenagers, men with AIDS, or domestic abuse survivors, I passionately wanted to do what I could.

What did I learn from volunteering? It broadened my perspective, expanded my awareness of a wider variety of people, and made me realize how fortunate and blessed I am to be able to help others.

Why should you volunteer? Because you can help yourself as well as others. The rewards are endless: You'll benefit from seeing how other people live and think, reap the joy of building new relationships, and discover how different genders, ethnicities, and generations feel and act as real people, not as stereotypes or assumptions. Volunteering gives you opportunities to explore other activities, occupations, interests, and even other parts of the world. It also gives you a bigger external mission to focus on and at the same time, the satisfaction of knowing you are contributing to the well-being of others.

Over the next several pages, I'll share a few of my volunteering adventures to give you an idea of the range of these experiences, the people I worked with, the joys and pitfalls that come with the territory, and some lessons I learned. As with everything in life, not every volunteering activity I attempted was a complete success, and that is to be expected. For every failure, there were also many rewarding triumphs and breakthroughs, large and small. And even the failures produced profound insights for me.

I hope this chapter inspires you to try volunteering. And if you don't find your first, second, or even third attempt to be fulfilling, don't give up, because finding an organization whose mission you truly resonate with—and its ethos, politics, and people—can take time and patience. But once you do, it changes your life in ways you never imagined.

The Young Adult Group

When we lived in the Philadelphia suburb of Dresher in the 1960s, my husband Len and his friend Irv started a support group for young people with developmental disabilities. They ranged in age from nineteen to twenty-eight. Because they were generally not included by their peers in mainstream activities, they needed outlets for socialization. We were aware of this need because of friends who had a son with such disabilities. We'd chaperone these young adults, take them to dances, hold frank discussions about life and dating, and generally coach them on how to engage in appropriate social interactions. Their parents deeply appreciated these opportunities for these young people to engage in such activities and conversations. Many of our members were very functional, enjoyed dating, and even considered marriage as they grew older.

So often in our conscious and subconscious minds, we lump the developmentally disabled young and old into narrow groups, not realizing that in the process, we label and treat these people as if they do not have any brainpower or physical ability, that they are somehow "less-than." This discrimination becomes a vicious cycle; the more they're excluded from experiencing the everyday life their peers enjoy, the more likely they are to internalize this stigma, suffer low self-esteem, and be denied the opportunity to ever experience normalization in their lives. Over a lifetime, this damage to their bodies, souls, and psyches is incalculable.

Today in 2022, we are finally starting to value them as the quality workers and feeling people they are. In our Bainbridge Island Rotary Club, we recently hired a young woman to assist at the welcoming desk for our meetings. It was very evident that she enjoyed greeting the members, and we were delighted to have her. In fact, this wonderful woman, who is about twenty years old, took on additional duties and has now moved on to a higher-paying position with more responsibilities.

ANNE FRANK HOUSE

In the mid-1940s, Americans were becoming aware of the true extent of the horrors and tragedies of World War II. I was about twenty when *Anne Frank: The Diary of a Young Girl* was published in the US in 1952, and I read the book with sadness at the wasted lives of Anne and much of her family, who died while in Nazi concentration camps during the Holocaust.

Most of us are familiar with the tragic story of Anne Frank, a young girl whose fate continues to remind today's generations of the senseless horror of genocide and war. Many tourists, including me, have visited the Anne Frank House in Amsterdam, Netherlands, where she and her family hid for two years from the Nazis.

In 1988, I had the opportunity to meet with many charitable, like-minded individuals who wanted to create a museum in Old City to raise awareness of the Holocaust in Philadelphia. We formed bylaws, established a nonprofit, and even identified a property that would serve as an ideal site to disseminate knowledge and history to high schoolers, college students, and the public. In addition, we wanted to establish various educational programs and high-quality exhibits.

We also forged favorable connections with the organization representing the Anne Frank House, the site and now museum in the Netherlands where Miep Gies had helped hide Anne, her family, and others in the unused rooms above the office of Otto Frank, Anne's father. Miep was a Roman Catholic working as a secretary for Mr. Frank's business, which remained open under figurehead Christian management. From 1942 to 1944, Mrs. Gies procured food for the Frank family, brought them books and news of the outside world, and provided emotional support, such as bringing Anne her first pair of high-heeled shoes and baking a holiday cake for her.

I was very excited at the prospect of bringing a replica of the Anne Frank House to Philadelphia. I felt Old City was a perfect location because it is where America's founding fathers gathered to discuss the philosophic ideas that would form the cornerstone of American democracy and concept of equality. Above all, Philadelphia represents the birthplace of freedom from the type of persecution that cut short the lives of Anne and her family.

As the design phase and ensuing negotiations progressed, another Philadelphian, Irvin J. Borowsky, became interested in the project. Since Mr. Borowsky was a well-known publisher and philanthropist, we were all initially pleased to have him on the board. But it soon became apparent that he wanted to control many aspects of the museum, including the design and even its location. He also tried to use his financial strength to promote his views.

The Anne Frank House in Amsterdam. The building in the middle contained the Secret Annex, where Anne Frank and her family hid from the Nazis for two years until they were discovered. Anne died in the Bergen-Belsen concentration camp in 1945, but her extensive diaries and journals were preserved, revealing the hopes and dreams of a young girl who still believed in the good of humanity.

At a board meeting at his substantial offices, I became convinced that Mr. Borowsky, who had a reputation of being difficult to work with, did not have the best interests at heart of the board and the Anne Frank House supporters. It took another six months before the board realized that they could not go along with Mr. Borowsky's plans. Unfortunately, the entire project had to ultimately be abandoned.

Recently I found a note in my files from fellow board member Larry Metzman, who wrote, "Flo, when you're right, you're right—and you *were* right!" At the time, I did not feel very pleased about the outcome, and I remain very sad and disappointed that there is still no Anne Frank museum in Philadelphia.

AIDS INFORMATION NETWORK

When the AIDS crisis began in the early 1980s, I learned about the AIDS Information Network, a resource service for gay men in Philadelphia. At the time, I was a very close personal friend of the Network's board president, and he and I discussed the horrors of the AIDS crisis and what could be done about it. I saw what an urgent health issue this was (literally a matter of life and death), and I knew the board needed help, so I volunteered to serve. We provided training on handling HIV diagnoses, resources for medical assistance, legal referrals, housing references, and a general office in Old City to answer questions and provide support.

Several years after the Network began providing these services, many new groups had formed to serve the growing AIDS population. Since more information was now available in the public sector, our board felt the Network should merge with one or more of these groups. By joining forces and working together, we'd all be more efficient and better able to serve our clients and the community.

But the board president did not want to give up control. Given my close relationship with him, I was the one selected to broach this sensitive decision. So, over breakfast at the DoubleTree Hotel one morning, I suggested to him that a merger would be a good idea.

That was the end of our friendship! He was furious that I had even made this suggestion and that the board had collectively agreed. Ultimately, the merger did take place, but he never spoke to me again. I felt very bad about this because I lost a friend in the process, but in the end, it was to the advantage of the local community to move in that direction.

CENTER FOR PREVENTION OF DOMESTIC VIOLENCE

When I was living in Colorado Springs in 1999, I volunteered at the Center for Prevention of Domestic Violence, which provided advocacy, community education, counseling, court watch, and a crisis line. The Center's services were intended for local women, men, and children who were caught in cycles of violent family abuse.

To be accepted as a Center volunteer, I had to submit a notarized application, make a six-month commitment, and undergo an intensive three-month training course. Once I completed all this, I finally became a court-appointed special advocate. This position entailed accompanying a client (usually a woman) to the courthouse to obtain a restraining order against a husband, partner, or another individual to legally keep that person from contacting the abused client and inflicting further physical harm, mental abuse, and intimidation. I also interviewed women and men who visited the Center. If it was their first time, they were scared, nervous, angry, and bewildered, but they often came back to get repeat advice and continue their counseling.

The makeup of the clientele varied; they usually consisted of military spouses, single enlisted junior officers, and civilian residents. Colorado Springs is home to five major Army and Air Force military bases, which include about 40,000 uniformed and 13,000 civilian personnel as of 2019. Women especially are often treated unfairly in the military, whether they're enlisted or married to those who are.

One day, I read in the newspaper that a male officer had smashed a glass bottle in a woman's face, injuring her. The next day I was sitting at a desk in the Center's office when a petite, dark-haired woman with a heavily bruised face walked in, looking nervous. She began telling me her story, and I suddenly realized this was the very same person I'd read about in the morning newspaper. Her husband was an officer in the Air Force; needless to say, I was very distressed and surprised.

I tried to convince her to sign a restraining order against her husband, but she refused—like many domestic abuse survivors, she was too afraid of what might happen as a result. I suggested that she come back again for help. But I never saw her again, and I worried deeply about her for a long time afterward.

Not only did the Center work to get restraining orders, but it also provided a safe house for women in an undisclosed location. I felt great sympathy for these victims. Yes, they were victims! Many were struggling every day without the strength, courage, self-esteem, or finances to make a change. I often wondered how long these women had been enduring these horrible situations—were these dynamics something they had grown up with in some form? Coming from a home where no one had ever been abused or threatened emotionally or physically, I realized just how blessed I was. Of course, not everything had been perfect in my life, but still, I felt incredibly grateful for my relatively good fortune—as well as to have discovered an enormous need out there and how I could use my privilege to help a little, one person at a time.

HADASSAH

Hadassah is the largest international Jewish women's organization in the world. With chapters all over the globe, it supports and builds hospitals, funds ground-breaking medical research, and works with children and young adults in Israel. It is also known for its work in preventing discrimination and ensuring quality medical care for all its patients, regardless of gender, religion, or ethnicity.

I was invited to join the Colorado Springs chapter of Hadassah in 1999. Although I'd never been in the organization before, I was inveigled into helping a deteriorating chapter suffering from a lack of leadership, and I became its president the following year. Our primary function was to raise funds for research and facilities, so my job was to instill public excitement, awareness, and interest in our chapter to make it stronger. We put on engaging, informative programs for potential donors and volunteers about the organization's mission and the chapter's specific goals. With the help of some younger members, we were able to achieve our goals and I'm happy to report that the chapter continues to gain new members and raise funds to meet medical needs in Israel.

In 2005, I was invited to a Hadassah "Women in Finance" tour. We visited the New York Stock Exchange as well as the vaults at the Federal Reserve Bank of New York, where more than 6,000 tons of gold are stored for other nations. We also visited the then-new, innovative Bloomberg Tower and posed for a photo-

Our Hadassah Women in Finance group at the New York Stock Exchange in 2005.

graph standing before the famous Charging Bull statue in front of the NYSE. Not surprisingly, I was the only woman wearing a hat!

Hadassah also offered me the opportunity to go to Israel for a fantastic tour. It was not my first visit there, but with their excellent guides, I discovered why the government was building its massive Separation Wall and how the country's population was becoming more diverse with the recent influx of Ethiopians. I also marveled at the beauty of its Mormon Temple (Church of Jesus Christ of Latter-Day Saints) overlooking the Grove of Olives in Tel Aviv-Yafo and numerous ancient and newly discovered archaeological findings.

Even after moving from Colorado to Seattle in 2012, I continue to be a member of Hadassah and occasionally attend events.

WOMEN'S PRISONS IN COLORADO

During my final years in Pennsylvania, my second husband Larry started a group that made weekly visits to Jewish prisoners in the now-closed State Correctional Institution-Graterford, a maximum-security facility about thirty miles northwest of Philadelphia. Many incarcerated men get very few visitors, and that isolation from and lack of socialization with the outside world can deeply damage their mental and physical health. Once their sentences are over and it's time for them to reenter society after years or sometimes decades of prison life, they often simply aren't ready for the enormous stress, discrimination, and overstimulation they'll encounter "on the outside."

I was already familiar with some of these issues from volunteering with the Philly Project, which helped incarcerated men apply for parole and find job placements in the community after their release. But the odds were unfairly stacked against them because a crime bill passed by Congress in 1994 banned all prisoners from receiving federally subsidized Pell Grants, denying them the opportunity to earn a college degree or even a high school diploma—and the latter is necessary to apply for most entry-level jobs. (The education ban wasn't lifted until 2021.) Nor were governments offering any work experience to help inmates reenter society and become financially independent at that time.

After we relocated to Colorado Springs, Larry continued this work at correctional facilities and prisons there, visiting Jewish prisoners once or twice a month. In 1999, I volunteered to go to the now-closed Colorado Women's Correctional Facility in Cañon City, about an hour's drive from our home. Here, I led monthly classes on Jewish history or the Bible for imprisoned women. (If truth be told, most of the prisoners' visitors really consisted of parishioners from local church groups coming to entertain by singing.) Frankly, the incarcerated women who attended these classes were just happy to have someone—anyone—visit them, whether they were Jewish, Christian, or atheist.

One year, included in the group of three or four women who attended my class was Jill Coit, an infamous "black widow" (a term for wives who kill their husbands). She had been married eleven times to nine different men and convicted of murdering at least one of them. She was very good-looking—and the most manipulative person I have ever met in my life.

There was also a beautiful, intelligent young woman who was perhaps only twenty years old, who had had all four of her children taken away from her. Yet another woman was only eighteen years of age. It was heartbreaking to see just how young these incarcerated women were and sense the suffering they'd endured in their very short lives.

You are never allowed to ask a prisoner what crime they're incarcerated for or any personal questions, so I did not know much about them unless they chose to tell me. My strongest motivation was to simply be a listening ear for these women, who desperately wanted to speak with someone from the outside world. How eagerly they looked forward to my visits.

One day a friend from New Jersey came to visit us in our new Colorado home. I told her that I was going to the women's prison that Monday night. She was curious, never having set foot in one, and she asked if she could go with me. After she submitted the required proof of identification to accompany me, we met with several women during our visit. Normally, we don't shake hands, hug anyone, or have any physical contact with the inmates. But on this particular visit, one inmate lightly hugged me and brushed up against my friend as we were finishing our seventy-five-minute session.

On the following Saturday morning, my friend frantically called me, having returned home from her visit with me. She exclaimed, "Florence, I was just watching a movie on television, and they were talking about the 'Black Widow.' Is that really the woman I met? Oh my God! I'm scared to death!" It turned out to be Jill Coit who had touched my dismayed friend.

Despite Coit's notoriety, this was not a high-security facility, I could walk by myself into the room where I met the prisoners and not have a guard accompanying me. I volunteered here for many years and found it to be very satisfying work.

In 2001, I worked to set up classes at the new Denver Women's Correctional Facility. Soon I was granted permission by the Colorado Department of Corrections to design and teach two programs, one on self-esteem and the other in basic finance. I'd visit the facility once a week for the four-week session. I did not give my students homework, but I believe the classes were well received as the women faithfully returned every week (either that or they had nothing more exciting to do, which of course was also quite possible).

The self-esteem course was especially needed. Many of the female inmates had been incarcerated once or twice before. Most were in prison because their husbands or boyfriends had taken part in illegal, violent activities, and these women had gotten entangled in these crimes by association or forced circumstances, such as driving a getaway car during an armed robbery or running drugs. It is almost impossible to comprehend how low these women's sense of self-worth really was, inured as they were by a lifetime of physical, emotional, and sexual abuse, often starting from early childhood. Having grown up in environments where their basic needs for security, love, and validation were frequently ignored and repeated cruelty was normalized, these women stood little chance of overcoming being controlled by others, especially males. But once they began learning about (or rediscovering) self-esteem, they could then begin to make small goals, work toward achieving them, take pride in themselves, and build confidence.

Similarly, I started my course in basic finance by drawing a picture of a check on a blackboard, complete with all the lines, and then describing how to fill it out. Does that sound unusual? Way too simple? Yes, it was an eye-opener for me to meet these women who were deprived of the most basic financial knowledge—and thus independence and self-reliance. It pained me so much to see women so deeply under the wiles, direction, and control of their abusers that it made me want to spend more time helping them. I continued teaching courses at the women's prison until I moved to Seattle.

USP Florence ADMAX

Because of Larry's work at Graterford, the Philadelphia branch of the Religious Society of Friends (also known as the Quakers) alerted him to the needs of inmates in USP Florence ADMAX, a super-maximum-security prison in Florence, Colorado. Starting around 2000, Larry and I began traveling to this prison, also known as *ADX Florence* or just *ADX*, about every other month for several years to interact with prisoners who rarely got visitors.

Known informally as the Alcatraz of the Rockies, ADX is one of the most secure prisons in the entire United States, far more so than the more common maximum-security prison. Only the most dangerous, violent, and disruptive prisoners are confined here, and most have life sentences or are considered threats to national security if they were to escape or be released. Almost 95 percent of the inmates here are transfers with histories of violence at other prisons. Larry sometimes visited a Japanese man here who was worried that he might be extradited back to Japan where the punishment and conditions were much worse.

Among the ADX's most notorious residents are the Boston Marathon bomber Dzhokhar Tsarnaev; the Oklahoma City bomber Terry Lynn Nichols; and Joaquín "El Chapo" Guzmán, the Mexican cartel leader infamous for his unprecedented drug trafficking that reaped billions of dollars in profits, laundered money on a gargantuan scale, and caused the deaths of countless Americans from drug addiction and overdoses—not to mention Guzmán's own two prior prison escapes.

The ADX's cells are made from poured concrete, as are the beds, desks, and stools. Inmates are isolated twenty-three hours a day and allowed only one hour out of their cells for exercise in a tiny concrete pit that's designed so they don't know their location even within the prison (to prevent their planning an escape). Exercise privileges may be taken away for the slightest infraction, such as a raised voice. Lights, radios, and mirrors in the rooms are optional, but televisions are very rare, reserved only for good behavior—but even then, they're seldom awarded. During at least their first three years in ADX, inmates are not allowed to communicate or interact with other inmates in any way. Food is brought to their cells by the guards, and the inmates always eat their meals alone.

To get permission to visit a prisoner at the ADX, Larry and I had to fill out extensive forms and undergo thorough background checks. Once we were approved to

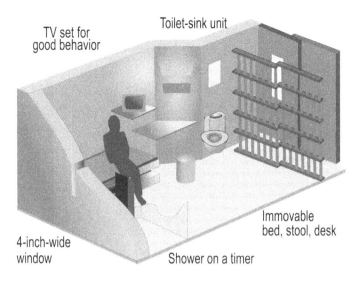

TV set for
good behavior

Toilet-sink unit

4-inch-wide
window

Shower on a timer

Immovable
bed, stool, desk

*An artist's illustration of how a cell inside the ADMAX is configured,
with every detail designed to maximize security. The cell measures seven feet by twelve feet.*

visit, we had to apply for a specific date at least a month in advance. The town of Florence was forty miles from our home in Colorado Springs; in good weather, the ride would take about an hour, but when conditions were bad, it took much longer.

Once we approached this very low, sprawling concrete structure, we immediately knew we were being observed very closely by innumerable security cameras and guards. After passing through the first set of gates, we'd register at the front desk and then be escorted to a set of lockers where we'd leave behind purses and empty our pockets of keys, money, everything. A guard would then lead us through the next set of gates and down a long hallway. Then finally, we passed through the third set of gates that opened onto a very large room. As we entered, we could see six Plexiglass-windowed visitor booths positioned side by side. A single chair sat in front of each window, and there was a telephone for communication. A guard would escort me to a booth, where I'd sit down in the chair while Larry was led to a separate booth. Then we'd await the arrival of our separate inmates, whom we'd talk to by phone while looking at each other through the clear window.

When Larry and I first started coming to the ADX, we had no idea who we might be seeing. If a prisoner didn't want a visitor, he could refuse the visit. I recall only twice when a prison-assigned inmate would not come to the window when we came, but others were available who could be summoned instead.

Generally, I'd wait about fifteen minutes; then the rear door behind the glass booth would open. A prisoner would shuffle in, led by a guard, his hands bound in front with handcuffs and his legs shackled in short ankle chains that were also attached to his handcuffs. The first time I ever saw an ADX inmate walk in and sit down to face me in the booth was a shock—to see how tied up and weighted down he was, like a dangerous wild animal. The guards would stay in the booths or stand just outside the prisoner's door the entire time of the visit. I would have received the prisoner's name from the front desk, so I'd say hello, address him by name, and state my own first name. Sometimes the inmates were surprised to see a woman.

Many times, prisoners did not start speaking to me immediately. And it was not because these men felt awkward or uncomfortable; they were seasoned adults living in a world they knew they'd made for themselves. They did not seek sympathy from me, nor were they sensitive to any judgment I might have toward them. Perhaps they were simply feeling awkward and maybe had almost forgotten how to speak to another human being, considering how their extreme solitary confinement defined every aspect of their current existence.

On these visits, I did not ask many questions since the men almost always wanted to do the talking. All I gave them was my first name, and mostly I just listened. Sometimes they asked about current news. One wanted me to send him magazines; of course, that wasn't allowed. They were very literate, some were highly intelligent, and they usually spoke quietly—never yelling or acting out. We'd generally talk for forty-five minutes or up to an hour at a time.

I learned that some inmates hadn't had any visitors for six months, a year, or even two years. None of them were stupid or ignorant. One prisoner talked about how he could get out by learning about the law, and he'd recite entire pages from law books to me from memory, with nothing in his hands but the telephone. He was eager to express his legal position to anyone who would listen, which was quite understandable given his circumstances.

You may wonder if I was ever afraid to be here, surrounded by such deeply hardened criminals, terrorists, and murderers. I was not, as guards were always present and prisoners were restricted behind the protective windows in the booths. It was a wonder to hear their stories, although I doubt they were all true—otherwise, how could a person end up in such a place?

One man whom I visited more than once told me about life in the Los Angeles neighborhood where he was from. His brothers had all been in a prison as well, and one or two might still have been there. He told me that being in a gang was just a normal part of growing up in his town—necessary, even, to make a living, get food to eat, and gain protection from other gangs. He and his brothers joined gangs at early ages, which meant stealing food, robbing people, and even murdering them if that meant surviving themselves. This man never excused himself or said he was sorry for his actions.

Isolation is very damaging physically and mentally to the individual. Humans are an intensely social species; cut off that socialization, and we will literally die. A prisoner may cut or starve himself, attempt suicide, become incoherent, or worse. The US prison system is not built on the concept of compassion, caring, or true rehabilitation; nor do these facilities properly prepare inmates to reenter society or the workplace. Part of the problem lies in the fact that many smaller prisons are run by private companies instead of state governments; such privately managed prisons are first and foremost built to house inmates and make money, not to repair and offer hope to someone who has taken a wrong turn.

And because the United States has the highest incarceration rate in the world, its prisons are usually bursting at the seams with more individuals than the system can handle. We need to do more in this country to not just lock people up and throw them away. So much needs to be done—and could be. Once a person lands in prison, there is usually little outside help or intervention available to them. A huge bureaucratic legal system makes the rules, and so does the prison warden who must follow them.

I also observed jarring differences between state and federal prisons. For instance, nonfamily visitors to state prisons like the women's correctional facility I volunteered at in Cañon City tended to be from churches or smaller community organizations, with more entertainment-oriented goals like singing, dancing, and other recreational activities. These types of visitors and activities are absolutely necessary to provide badly needed joy and spiritual fulfillment. But I often felt more useful when I could teach, and I wish more classes and programs on basic life skills could be offered to inmates. These state facilities often felt like such "loose prisons" in comparison to their tighter-security federal counterparts, which I believe made it easier for them to host these constructive programs. But really, why can't federal prisons be granted some of these same priorities? After all, humans are humans, with universal needs, issues, and basic rights regardless of where they are.

Certainly, those in the ADX are rarely released and rehabilitated, as it is the most extreme of prisons in terms of the type of inmate and level of security. But precisely because its solitary confinement is so absolute, I felt glad that these inmates could at least occasionally see a pleasant face for a short time. Many of them had not seen relatives, children, friends, or anyone else other than prison guards and staff for years. Some of the men always thanked me for coming.

8

SILVER PLANET

A Call and a Need ~ Getting Up and Running ~
A Lesson Learned—But Still a Need

I cannot tolerate people taking advantage of the vulnerable.
— Florence Klein —

By 2007, I was seventy-three and living in a spectacular home with expansive views of the Air Force Academy, Pikes Peak, and the Rocky Mountains in Colorado Springs. But the joy I took in seeing this beauty contrasted with the pain I felt in the pit of my stomach whenever I thought about older people who were being taken advantage of by scammers. (I refer to older people as "elders" in this book—see the Ageism chapter for an explanation.) It seemed to me that they could not easily access resources to get reliable, trustworthy help. Perhaps, I thought, if they were able to call for advice over the telephone, they might not be as vulnerable.

A CALL AND A NEED

At that time, the sheer numbers of bogus phone calls and emails flooding wealthy countries from scammers in poorer nations like Nigeria were landing weekly in the news and other media. Radio stations and newspapers reported how clever and deceptive these thieves were in targeting elders, asking for their help, and requesting money. A scammer might set up the situation by pleading, "I just found out that my father had left me $75,000, but it was tied up in the tax office of the Nigerian Central Office. Until I can come up with $10,000 to pay the tax, I cannot get the funds released and I need the money for my wife's cancer treatment. If you could help me with $8,000 of the tax, I will send you back $20,000 by wire as soon as I get the money."

Another scam might go like this: "Your niece called and she's stuck in Norway. She had her purse ripped off and now she has no money to get home; she needs to go to the embassy and get a new passport and $880 to get a plane ticket for home." These callers would sound friendly and sincere, and they'd quickly begin building relationships with their sympathetic victims, who were lonely at home, eager to talk to anyone, wanted to help, and were easy prey for their ruses. Once the victims went to their banks several times to withdraw funds to send to foreign addresses, the local bankers, who knew their customers, would alert them and their families. After finding out that they'd been scammed, these elders often felt so ashamed and humiliated that they refused to speak to anyone about their losses, which only compounded their misery.

My nascent idea to help these vulnerable people by providing a telephone service set me in motion. I reasoned that if an elder had a nonjudgmental, supportive hotline they could anonymously turn to, many of their answers might be addressed immediately, and that would save them from losing potentially thousands of dollars in life savings. Ever an action visionary, I drafted a program and sprang into action. I could address the financial questions as I still had my own broker-dealer company, American Classic Financial. I contacted professionals like attorneys, physicians, insurance brokers, accountants, and financial advisors, who would serve as referrals for these elders' questions. The advisors were receptive to this arrangement since they would receive an opportunity to develop new clients and be able to address the elders' questions.

Knowing that I would need additional technical help with this venture, I hired a friend to obtain the necessary business licenses and organize this effort under my direction. Unfortunately, she was unable to continue because of illness. I then became involved with family affairs and had to set this idea aside for a while.

But for the next six months, I continued thinking about the plight of elders. I read about a new website that had recently become popular called MySpace. I thought, *How about having my own site called MySeniors?* Once I realized that the Internet was destined to become the communication super-highway of the future, I began to look for direction from several consultants and a technology friend, Manuel Martin, to discuss this idea.

It didn't take me long to realize that many elders were really frustrated with using the Internet, myself included. We were still in the relatively early days of the Web, and most older people were not using it or visiting websites. (Which seems amazing now when we realize how quickly the Internet became so popular and necessary in daily life.) With a mind-boggling range of content instantly available in a form that humans had never seen before, the Internet was both profoundly exciting and confusing for users of all ages. And its incredible power to open new realms of knowledge, opportunity, and networking for people all over an inequitable world provided easy ways for some to take advantage of others anonymously on a global scale.

Not only were elders especially afraid of scams, but they were often stymied by a lack of credible content and information they could trust, especially regarding fraud and general resources. I decided to provide that space—even though I myself had no tech experience other than using a Windows PC computer. Plus, I had a secretary, so I didn't interact much with the Internet either.

When I began telling people about my idea, the first reaction I often received was, "Oh, Florence, seniors don't use the Internet." That was 2006—fewer than twenty years ago! A reporter from the *Colorado Gazette* asked me, "Why a website for seniors? They don't visit the Internet as much as other age groups." I responded to her question by stating, "I want to empower more seniors to communicate and interact more effectively in today's highly technical world. The use of the Internet by the fifty-five-plus age group is growing, especially with the baby boomers aging and using the Web. Our tagline is 'Inform, inspire, interact.'"

With that, she wrote a front-page article about my new company.

Getting Up and Running

With my own funds, I started the company by purchasing the domain name MySeniors.com and hired a web designer. It took about a year to get this venture organized and start a team. During this time, I hired an operations person, a tech advisor, and two or three others to populate the site with content and get it up and running.

True to our mission, our site was exceptionally informative, with high-quality columns on nutrition, healthcare, and lifestyle issues, as well as resource listings on broader topics like legislation, housing, and social services. Visitors could sign up for free with their name and a password to establish a user account and become a member. Once visitors became members, they could ask us questions and get them answered on our website. Since we were aware of the latest scams and phishing trends from law enforcement, FBI reports, trusted media outlets, and other reliable sources, we instituted Silver Scam Alerts that we'd send out weekly to our members via email to warn them as early as possible.

This was a lot of work, but it was particularly gratifying when we'd receive a comment like this: "*I am so glad I received the scam alert as I was about to send money to a man who sounded so sincere, but then I read the alert. Thank you.*"

Once we started getting more visitors to our site, we received very positive reviews, not only from people in the United States but also from Canada and the UK. Despite site traffic increasing in the beginning, our ratings on Google did not attract enough new bona fide members. And similar websites began sprouting as

LOCAL WOMAN STARTS SITE FOR SENIOR CITIZENS

Aims to offer content they can trust, involve them in technology

BY CAROL MCGRAW
THE GAZETTE

When Florence Klein decided to start a Web site for senior citizens, she didn't mess around. "I had a big vision, so I started big," the 74-year-old Colorado Springs woman says matter-of-factly.

Klein launched silverplanet .com in April, but the site looks as if it had been an online mainstay, with a range of information not seen on even more mature sites that target seniors. It has blogs and columns on entertainment, consumer news, health care, lifestyles and relationships, book and movie reviews, crossword puzzles and recipes.

What's not there, she says is, "advocacy, promotion of particular religions, scams, lobbying, politics."

"I wanted a place that seniors could trust," she says.

Klein is the first to admit that she is no techie, but she has a lifetime of business experience to bring to her role as Silver Planet's founder and chief executive.

She grew up in Pennsylvania, earned a degree in marketing and management from the Wharton School at the University of Pennsylvania, and became one of the first female stockbrokers in Philadelphia. She was also a real estate developer. About 20 years ago she started American Classic Financial, of which she is CEO. She moved to Colorado about 13 years ago. She has three children and six grandchildren.

Question: Why did you start silverplanet.com?

Answer: Traveling around the country, I've talked to a lot of seniors who have told me that they are really frustrated with the Internet. They are especially afraid of scams and can't find information they can trust. There's a lack of credible content. So I decided to provide it.

Q: Why a Web site for seniors? They don't visit the Internet as much as other age groups.

A: I want to empower more seniors to communicate and

SEE KLEIN • PAGE 3

At 74, Florence Klein is a busy woman and founder of www.silver planet.com, a Web site designed for seniors. The site provides information on a wide range of topics. She plans to set up community events where seniors can get together.

BRYAN OLLER,
THE GAZETTE

KLEIN: Silverplanet.com is an international site

FROM PAGE 1

interact more effectively in today's highly technical world. The use of the Internet by the 55-plus group is growing, especially with the baby boomers aging and using the Web. Our tag line is "Inform, inspire, interact."

Q: How long did it take to set everything up?

A: We worked on it for a year and a half. We started with a business plan and talked to consultants. Since it's a large site, we needed to get a lot of people and technology in place, design and graphics.

Q: How large is your staff?

A: Counting myself, we have seven full-time and seven part-time, all paid positions. We have freelance columnists and use some syndicated material.

Q: What are the business challenges and how are you meeting them?

A: The technology changes so quickly and you have to be up to speed in programming and codes — also increasing traffic and monetizing the site. We need to start getting revenue now. We are talking to some big pharmaceutical companies and others.

As far as traffic, we have been using word of mouth, links, publicity, e-mail. We are moving into more established public relations work in different cities. We aren't just a local site; we are international.

Q: Are you getting visitors?

A: We are moving along and people are starting to become aware of us. Traffic has increased 600 percent in the past six weeks. But I'd rather not give figures.

Q: You recently received a $10,000 grant from the Rose Community Foundation in Denver. Explain what you are doing.

A: The grant will be used to create a Silver Ambassadors Program, which will get senior citizen Web users away from computer screens and into the community for special events sponsored by Silver Planet. What bothers me a lot is so many seniors become so lonesome and isolated.

When people get older they need to be part of the regular community and connect with others. We'll have programs on all kinds of things, from the arts to finances to guided-travel groups.

Q: How much has it cost to start the Web site?

A: It has been a large investment. I don't care to say how much. But we want it to be profitmaking. But we don't want to compromise on integrity to get there.

Q: How much does it cost to subscribe to your site?

A: It is free. You don't have to pay at all.

Q: What are some of your favorite features?

A: My favorite is the Silver Star stories about extraordinary, inspiring seniors who embrace a new view on aging. We give an annual Silver Star Award based on the person who receives the most online votes. (Silver Planet is now choosing the 2008 winner, and gearing up for the 2009 contest. People can go to the Web site to nominate themselves or others for 2009.)

We have six bloggers and other contributors. We have a resident poet, known as the Silver Sage. There's an advice column called Crabby and Blabby, and a caregiver blog, a recipe doctor, nutrition, finance, and another on aging called Dear Ellie.

We have a scam alert so our members know what is happening and can beware of people who try to take advantage of seniors. That really gets me. We have a lot of original content and an editorial review board to choose everything that is printed on the Web site to make sure it is up to our standards.

Q: Have you thought of retiring?

A: Never. I feel ageless. But ideas about retirement are changing and we believe that there is a different approach to aging. It's not sitting in a rocking chair. It's being active, expanding your horizons and being helpful to others. That's my mantra.

Questions and answers are edited
for space and clarity.

An article about Silver Planet in the Colorado Springs–based newspaper, The Gazette, *January 30, 2009.*

their creators figured out that ever more baby boomers, with their aging parents and older siblings, were seeking advice to help one of the fastest-growing demographics in America.

Realizing that the name MySeniors carried a negative connotation of ageism, we changed our domain name to Silver Planet. We also introduced a direct phone line service that was available fifteen hours a day to receive calls, as well as an emergency line linked to a resource—much like my original idea. People would call with questions, and we might refer them to a professional caregiver near them or a local housing facility.

My daughter Karen introduced many innovative programs to Silver Planet, including the Silver Concierge, which provided information on services, care, and resources for seniors and others to make the transition from hospitals or rehabilitation facilities back to their homes, along with follow-up by home care specialists. To this day, this remains a much-needed service.

The Silver Stars program was a favorite of mine. In the course of our work, we met with many providers, so we heard many stories about remarkable individuals. Eventually, we began soliciting our members to cast their votes every month for an elder over the age of sixty-five who was extraordinary and inspiring and had done an unusual deed or embraced a new view of aging. Our board would then review these nominations and vote on this Silver Star of the Month. By the end of 2008, we were discussing the Silver Star of the Year.

We had a great deal of original content that we paid to create, as well as an editorial review board that chose what we posted on the website to make sure it met our high standards. And then we released this premium material to members without charging a subscription fee—which was a huge mistake.

Faced with looming needs for significant external financing, I hired a Wharton School graduate as an advisor to obtain additional funding, but she was not successful. With six or seven paid employees, various fees, and different technology strategies, our costs were growing exponentially. We did receive a $10,000 grant from the Rose Community Foundation that we used to establish a Silver Ambassadors program to encourage seniors to get out of their homes and attend special Silver Planet Ambassadors programs throughout the Denver area. But such outside funding was the exception, not the rule.

A Lesson Learned—But Still a Need

In 2011, with no additional funding coming in, I cut staff and attempted to keep the website alive. However, with changes in fast-moving technology, the need to make constant site improvements and updates, and the drain on my finances, I finally had to close the site when I relocated to Seattle in 2013. Nonetheless, I still meet people who had used Silver Planet and loved it. It was very hard for me to give it up, and I continue to feel that pain because it met so many concrete needs that affect day-to-day lives.

This outcome is exceptionally sad because I believe that the need that I had acted upon in 2007 is even more acute today. In today's fragmented world, especially in the wake of the COVID-19 pandemic, it sometimes seems more difficult to make meaningful, genuine connections, even if technologically we're more linked than ever (although granted, given Silver Planet's web presence, being online does have its advantages).

This is on top of the physical isolation that elders in car-centric America already live with—many do not drive and thus cannot easily get out to see friends, run errands, and participate in social activities. Families often live in places too distant from one another and seldom visit, adding to the loneliness. We're living longer and healthier lives, but as our numbers grow exponentially in the United States, one wonders about the quality of this longer life.

Still, opportunities abound if one seeks them. For instance, several years ago, I needed help setting up some accounting records. I hired a lovely sixteen-year-old female student who came to my home. In between our work chores, I shared stories and books about experiences in other countries as well as maps with her, and she told me about her ideas and perspectives. We exchanged many wonderful conversations on numerous topics, and the whole experience was both delightful and productive. I look forward to doing this again. To that end, we need to create and foster more opportunities for elders and younger people to spend time with each other in all sorts of ways. They could travel together, live in intergenerational housing, and help each other more where they live and work. I discuss this more in the chapter on ageism.

In the end, I do not feel Silver Planet was a failure. We did help an untold number of people, and the experience afforded me opportunities to see my own deficits. As a visionary, I found that I cannot be an operator, I am not a details person, I cannot be a marketer, and I may not always be the best person to evaluate prospective employees and contractors. It was all an enormous lesson!

9
LIFE CHANGES

Marriage ~ Larry Karlin ~
Moving West ~ My Fifth Career

In my eighties, I am still actively embarking on new personal and professional adventures.
— Florence Klein —

I must admit that, in some ways, marriage is not something I've excelled at in life. I was always a woman driven by a desire to forge a life outside of the home, have an ambitious career, and raise a successful family, but relationships with spouses have been difficult. As I've mentioned before, I knew when I married Len that I was becoming a wife at too young of an age, but I did not want to dash my mother's hopes that I would settle down with a nice Jewish boy. It wasn't that I disliked Len; I simply had other goals than what society expected of me. Getting married at twenty was not a priority for me.

Since I was the primary breadwinner in my first marriage rather than my husband, you might wonder if those reversed power roles played a role in our marital dynamics. Len, for his part, was always astonishingly open-minded and very supportive of my unusual career. We had so much trust in our relationship that he never questioned my overnight trips entertaining clients in New York or holding evening appointments. He was very proud of my real estate dealings, but he never had any real say in those business decisions. But I can honestly say that he truly loved me and was a wonderful, attentive father to our children.

It also helped that we were quite independent people, and comfortable doing things both separately and together. He was never content working just in his family's grocery business, which he had returned to in our early years of marriage only out of a sense of duty after his father died and his brother asked him to come in as a partner. So, he pursued his own interests, such as getting a private pilot's license, going to graduate school, and even volunteering in the Peace Corps for several years. He sometimes wanted me to go with him during these overseas placements, but I did not want to uproot the children from our life in the States, plus I had my own business enterprises to attend to in Philadelphia.

Like many couples, we gradually drifted apart, living our separate lives so much that we almost didn't notice. It wasn't that we fought or argued; Len once observed that "I simply outgrew him," and that was true—I was so busy and creative that I simply hadn't noticed the garden needed watering. While I loved entertaining friends, traveling with family, and celebrating holidays and birthdays with loved ones, I now realize that we had grown apart.

I was never unhappy enough to ask for a divorce. As I mentioned earlier in Chapter 2, Len simply came to me one day in 1989 requesting one, and I did not resist. Looking back on it, I believe we should have divorced fifteen years earlier so Len could have been free to live his own life sooner. I think I had been trying to keep the situation steady, remain compassionate, and not hurt him, but it was a mistake in the long run.

LARRY KARLIN

In 1998, I met a man named Larry Karlin through a friend. As I related in the earlier chapter about volunteering, he and I shared a common interest in helping prison inmates, and he had started a group that made weekly social visits to Jewish prisoners at the now-closed State Correctional Institution-Graterford near Philadelphia. Eventually, we decided to get married, and we moved from my beloved hometown out west to start a new life in Colorado Springs, since Larry already had a home in Vail and loved skiing.

My marriage to Larry soon started showing cracks. Initially, I had been attracted to him for his intelligence, meticulous appearance, and his desire to help people. He was exceptionally athletic and worked out constantly, to the extent that he had a home gym and basketball and tennis courts built in his backyard. It also helped that he was comfortable financially and had his own funds, so there were no issues with him being a gold digger.

Larry with my grandson Nathaniel in 1998.

But over time, I began noticing that he would never compliment me on my appearance, nor was he ever physically affectionate. He was always self-absorbed and could never bring himself to truly acknowledge me. And when we traveled as a family with my children, he often turned boorish, and his behavior was exceptionally embarrassing on a couple of memorable trips to Italy and China.

By now, you certainly know that I'm not the kind to be insecure or seek people's approval, but Larry's coldness truly chilled me. Once, I asked him gently, "How come you never touch my hand?" His immediate retort was, "Florence, you're just such a needy person." I was so shocked and hurt by this response, and it marked an indelible beginning of the end for us as a couple.

With our marriage rapidly deteriorating and divorce imminent, Larry severely injured his knee in 2010. I stayed on to take care of him throughout his knee operation and long rehabilitation. Finally, in 2012, we arranged a very amicable, simple divorce without expensive attorneys. I have never been fond of messy, public divorce proceedings that often divide children and families and leave both sides angry. Larry has since passed on, but to this day I still have a friendly relationship with Len, even though we have been apart for decades.

Moving West

While I was still with Larry in Colorado, waiting for the final divorce papers, my older daughter Karen, who lived on Bainbridge Island in Washington State, phoned me one day with a question: "What do you think about me running for Superior Court Judge in Kitsap County?" My immediate response was, "You have to do what your heart and passion tell you. If you run, I will help campaign for you." Karen decided she would run.

Soon, I was packing up my things, renting a storage unit nearby in Colorado Springs, and moving back to Philadelphia. Even as I was shipping two automobiles across the country and began renting an apartment, this question was uppermost in my mind: Just where did I want to live permanently now? At the time, Philadelphia is where I needed to be temporarily because my only sibling, Lew, was very ill with cancer and I wanted to be near him.

My heart was still very much in Philadelphia. After all, it was the place where I'd been born and raised, went to schools, got married, raised my children, and had spent most of my working life. But now that Karen was in the middle of a political campaign and I'd promised to help her, I kept flying across the country to Bainbridge Island. It was exciting to be so involved, dedicated, and energized in this work, getting up at six in the morning to drive in the dark to Bremerton to distribute flyers at the shipyard, knock on doors all over sprawling Kitsap County, and hang out at street corners with posters. I was ecstatic when she won the primary and progressed toward the November election, but unfortunately, she lost. I was heartsick but nonetheless extremely proud of my daughter.

And I was still at a crossroads and needed to decide where home would be. East or West? Colorado Springs was not an option for me, as I did not fit in there. But after Lew died, I chose to go west like so many pioneers and move to Washington to be closer to Karen. In 2012, I rented an apartment in downtown Seattle for its cultural arts, like the theater, orchestra, and ballet, and lived there for close to three years.

I felt the notorious "Seattle Chill"—a phenomenon experienced by many newcomers facing social isolation in an expanding, rapidly changing city benefiting from the financial prosperity of growing technology giants Amazon and Microsoft but still hanging on to old-money traditions. I realize now that I was a bit depressed in Seattle. I had lost my brother, divorced my second husband, was living alone in a new city not knowing anyone, and still feeling sad about Karen's campaign loss and the death of two very close friends.

But, never one to stay down or depressed for long, I moved across Puget Sound to Bainbridge Island in 2016. I have found it to be a true community full of quality people who exude warmth, friendship, and mutual interests.

MY FIFTH CAREER

At the age of eighty-two, I decided that I should start my fifth career. *It was about time*, I said to myself.

In the 1950s, I played the lead role in a local theater production of the play Night of January 16th.

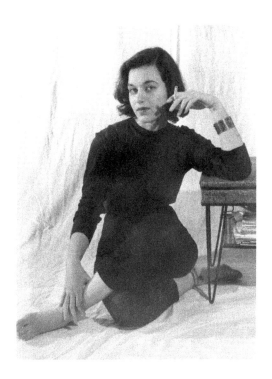

*Me at age eighteen in 1952, modeling for a
cigarette advertisement. I never smoked in real life.*

I looked into getting an agent who could help me get jobs modeling and acting. Actually, as I think about it, I have been modeling most of my adult life.

While in high school, I did some department store modeling while I was selling shoes at Strawbridge & Clothier. Some years later, I got an invitation from a clothes buyer at Strawbridge & Clothier to model bathing suits. She did not know that I was pregnant with my first child. I was quite small in early September as I strutted down the runway chuckling to myself about the beautiful secret I was carrying.

Then, when Len and I were living in Newport News, Virginia, I landed the lead role in a local theater production of *Night of January 16th*. But, between raising three children, being a stockbroker, running my own NASD brokerage firm, building and renovating historic real estate in Philadelphia, and starting a website for elders, I did not do much modeling or acting until I moved to Colorado Springs. There I enjoyed doing some charity fun shows and modeling a petite woman's business clothing line.

After checking out various agencies in Seattle in 2017, I was invited to join one in South Seattle. The modeling industry is sometimes a treacherous one, in which a woman can find herself unexpectedly in a pornographic situation or where nude photographs are being taken, which I fortunately avoided. Equipped with a great set of professional photos, a bona fide contract, and my old hatbox, I was ready!

Since I was now a professional, I had to prepare the wardrobe required for some roles and drag them to 6 AM shootings, as well as be made up with different cheekbones or unusual hairstyles. I got quite a few interviews, callbacks, and to my surprise, actual paid work. Once I spent two days playing a nurse for an Alzheimer's patient; another gig involved acting for a new movie series while wearing outrageous clothes.

I loved meeting the entirely new groups of people who were a part of these productions. Almost all the women and men I met during the long filming days, whether they were producers, photographers, leads, or others, I found friendly, interesting, and fun. The specialists, gymnasts, and young single moms looking to make extra money while worrying if filming would be finished in time for them to get home before the school bus arrived represented a new slice of life for me. Some men who recognized me after the first time we met on other jobs were interested in me as a romantic friend, but I was not.

Me visiting the Taj Mahal during a Rotary International trip in 2015. I was always interested in the history and culture of India, and this journey fulfilled a lifelong dream.

10

AGEISM

Exactly, What Is Ageism? ~ A Lifetime of Ageism in America ~
Ageism and Employment ~ What We Must Change ~
Aging and Housing ~ Intergenerational Housing ~
Aging and Courage ~ What We Can Do to Stop Being Ageist

Youth is everywhere in place.
Age, like woman, requires fit surroundings.
— Ralph Waldo Emerson —

We have time to grow old—the air is full of our cries.
— Samuel Beckett —

What is the meaning of the word *old*? As in *Oh, you're old*.

I have always felt that the word *old*, when referring to someone who is of a certain age, starts very young. I never considered my Grandma Ida old. Yes, I was aware that she was older than I was, but I never thought of her as incapable or unable to take charge of her life. To me, Ida was advancing in age just as I was advancing in years, but she certainly wasn't senile or incompetent.

An active woman, she sold tablecloths, which she delivered to her friends by walking to their homes. Even when she was in her nineties, she was determined that no one know she was partially blind, and so she pushed a baby carriage in front of her, keeping her dignity intact.

We often blurt out the word *old* carelessly, not realizing its negative effects. I personally believe that this concept moves through the years with you. Even now, at eighty-eight, I do not consider myself old. But it is all relative: We all know the thirty-year-old who perpetually seems psychologically stuck in place, or people who regard themselves with paralyzing pessimism: "Oh, I'm fifty and there's nothing more to life."

In America, our attitudes toward aging and ageism profoundly shape how we regard ourselves and treat others of all ages. The white, Western notion of aging is so different from how elders are regarded in China, Korea (which even has a special celebration to honor people entering their sixth decade), Africa, Greece, India, and Indigenous peoples. What can we learn from them?

Exactly What Is Ageism?

First, let's define the term because ageism differs from just "being older."

The Merriam-Webster dictionary describes ageism as "prejudice or discrimination against a particular age group and especially the elderly." The American psychiatrist and gerontologist Robert Butler believed that ageism is a "process of systematic stereotyping or discrimination against people because they are old, just as racism and sexism accomplish with skin colour and gender. Ageism allows the younger generations to see older people as different than themselves; thus, they subtly cease to identify with their elders as human beings." Even the *2021 Global Report on Ageism*, published by the World Health Organization, described ageism as "an important social determinant of health that has been largely neglected until now."

It's not just younger people who practice ageism toward elders; it goes the other way too. Older people sometimes discriminate against youth, especially adolescents and children, denying them certain legal privileges such as the right to vote or consent to medical treatment. Ageism also assumes less obvious forms, especially in the language we use. Without even realizing it, we say well-meaning but condescending phrases like "Oh, you're so young," "You're too young for that," and "You don't know anything" without considering that person's innate wisdom, knowledge, and experience. Over time, these messages can be internalized by everyone in some form.

Elders also perpetuate ageism with themselves and one another. It often reflects our fear of physical and mental decline and the loss of independence as we face mortality. Sometimes it's easier to chalk up our struggles to "Oh, I'm just getting old" and just try to sweep it under the rug. And we might not want to admit how hard it is to accept ourselves or others—age can be an excuse for not attending to our health, well-being, and aspirations.

Ageism has more influence than we might imagine. It manifests in how we view and treat one another both individually and collectively. It makes a difference in housing, healthcare, community-building, social gatherings, and employment. People tend not to think about ageism as much as racism and feminism; it isn't discussed openly as much. But it's unmistakably powerful, especially when combined with other "isms" such as gender and race—a powerful force that all of us routinely underestimate, hidden in plain sight.

A Lifetime of Ageism in America

I believe we start to socially learn ageism at a very early age—probably as early as six or seven years. As children, how do we get introduced to elders? It may begin with our relationship with grandparents, aunts, uncles, or even great-grandparents. Did they seem "old" to you? What were your first experiences with the elders in your family? Were they kind and affectionate? More indulgent and fun than your parents? What kinds of activities did you do with them? Were they loving and supportive in a way that your parents were not? Did you look forward to seeing them?

Or were they cranky or distant? Were you warned to sit still and behave when you visited them? Did they or your parents seem tense when they were together? Were your elders polite to you but not really interested in who you were? Or did they positively shape you in ways your parents didn't? Or even raise you?

Much of our early social conditioning toward elders depends on how we see our parents and immediate family members treat them. Powerful stereotypes, strong impressions, and sweeping assumptions often prevail, but our attitudes can change as well. Americans tend to stay within their own age groups throughout their lives and often seem more uncomfortable mixing outside them than people in other cultures. Certainly, our housing practices tend to relegate elders as practically invisible.

Ageism reared its ugly head in some shocking ways during the 2020 COVID-19 pandemic. Coronavirus challenged just about every population on the planet, but its effects were especially cruel in the United States. Elders were not only the most medically vulnerable age group for contracting and dying from the virus, but they were even targeted on social media as expendable: One Texas lieutenant governor Tweeted that, with limited healthcare resources, grandparents would be willing to die to preserve the economy for their children and grandchildren. A California lawyer declared this population "generally expensive to maintain and not productive."

By and large, America is obsessed with youth, with intense consumerism and marketing directed toward hanging on to it for as long as possible. In a culture noted for its relatively few rites of passage, aging is regarded with fear, denial, scorn, and ridicule. Birthday parties celebrating a mere fourth decade might feature funereal, black crepe-paper decorations and even the appearance of a walker as a good-natured joke. By fifty, popular culture has pretty much pegged you as "over the hill." Retirement marks a major turning point, but many people are retiring later out of financial necessity or choice, sometimes in their seventies or eighties. Interestingly, by the time you reach seventy-five or eighty, attitudes start reversing. If you're lucky to reach ninety, you might even be revered.

Women bear an extra burden because society places so much emphasis on their physical appearance. In America as in many cultures, nothing is more appealing than a female in all her youthful, fertile sensuality. Once wrinkles and cellulite appear, women become more invisible, increasingly ignored, and sometimes signaled as less valued by society. Men become more distinguished; women wither.

In a *New York Times* article published in March 2020, Leslie Bennetts reviews Susan J. Douglas's book *In Our Prime: How Older Women Are Reinventing the Road Ahead*. Douglas writes about the age-phobic hysterical responses by women, who are so overwhelmed by the realities of getting older that they're resorting to Botox, facelifts, and other cosmetic products to forestall time. With American consumers spending more than 11.6 billion dollars annually on anti-aging products as of 2021, the battle against nature rages on.

In reading this review, I'm reminded of the cover of a *Time* magazine dated August 3, 1970, titled "Behavior: The Old in the Country of the Young." I have a copy of it in front of me and even though it was published fifty-three years ago, its sentiments eerily echo today's words: "a burden," "a drain on the economy," and "not attractive after thirty." The article also states the famous gerontologist Robert Butler saying that he "believes that in 25 or 30 years, ageism will be a problem equal to racism."

Is that true today in 2022? These sentiments are getting old, so to speak. Just when are we going to change them?

AGEISM AND EMPLOYMENT

Elders are working longer—the US Bureau of Statistics has projected that people aged sixty-five and older are the fastest-growing segment of the workforce. The reason is sometimes financial, but working also gives many people pleasure and a mission in life that vitally connects them to their community.

Despite this boom, there is no doubt that in many industries, older people are being passed over for opportunities in favor of younger counterparts. This starts from the age of fifty onward, especially with new positions or promotions. Older people are often stereotyped as being set in their ways, slower to perform tasks, and more resistant to change and feedback than their younger colleagues, who are prized for their energy, stamina, and willingness to work longer hours for less money. The social signals of ageism are many and sometimes not so subtle: *Aren't you overqualified for this role? You make (fill in the blank) age look good! So, when's the big retirement? You can't teach an old dog new tricks!*

Most tellingly, young people are also experiencing ageism in the workplace. Even people in their thirties are experiencing reverse ageism when they're passed up

for twenty-somethings because the latter is that much less expensive to hire, more adaptable to the velocity of the fast-paced tech sector, and relatively unhindered by family obligations. Ironically, those employers may reject the innovative ideas of those very same people because they're deemed "too young to know what's best."

In fact, a 2017 study published by the American Psychological Association found that 60 percent of older employees (such as baby boomers) in their sample described younger millennial colleagues negatively and that close to 30 percent of employees in their twenties and thirties had experienced reverse age discrimination. Other studies have reported young employees experiencing even higher levels of age-related discrimination, even though they often regard their older counterparts more positively.

While dissing the young is nothing new among older people, this keen interest in generational differences and how it manifests personally and professionally—or perceived to be—is a relatively new phenomenon. People of all ages are being more sharply labeled by the media and popular opinion until these simple stereotypes become not only socially acceptable but considered legitimate.

Our natural human propensity to generalize, classify, overlook, and dismiss what we want and ignore everything else is only amplified by the belief systems of the societies under which we're raised. We jump on the bandwagon of feeling superior to someone else, but these destructive consequences only increase our generational divides when we should be bridging them, learning from one another, and working together.

What We Must Change

As a nation with a swiftly growing elder population, we must pay more attention to ageism if we want to change our attitudes and shift public discourse. First, we need to consistently fund better research on the process of aging, especially now that people are living longer. What motivates this demographic? How and why are they developing second and third careers? How are their relationships evolving? What is the impact on their health and longevity? Improved data can help us better understand and address these issues.

Second, we must invest in effective strategies. What are the consequences of ignoring people as they age and not paying attention to their increased need for transportation and employment? How can we identify gaps in their welfare, housing, healthcare, and social services? How do we enact legislation to solve them?

And third, we must build a social movement to change the narrative around age and aging. The language that the media uses to describe people is powerful, often doing more harm than good. For instance, we should eliminate the word *senior*. The very term triggers stereotypes and attitudes that can lead to unwitting discrimination and perpetuation—feeble, crotchety, senile. What comes to mind when you think of senior centers, senior living, and senior discounts? Is a senior citizen somehow less of a human being than a nonsenior one?

The same is true with the relatively new term *Super Seniors*. It's well-intended, but it emphasizes a select group of exceptionally functional, active people and praises them for being a special, privileged class. This is at the expense of the much larger group of elders who are not as active and should have been encouraged by society the entire time leading up to their current age. Labeling people is never a good thing. The term also paints Super Seniors as a momentary feel-good story that ignores the larger, difficult realities of aging, and it misleads an audience into thinking that ageism is not as serious as other forms of discrimination.

Again, ageism goes both ways. When referring to children, teenagers, and adolescents, we unthinkingly toss around terms like *kids, just a child, going through a phase, juvenile, troubled, bratty,* and *tantrum* when we wouldn't use the same language if they were adults. Being aware of and respectful to an individual regardless of their age should be a lifelong practice.

Aging and Housing
A History

One topic near and dear to my heart is intergenerational housing. Before I discuss this, it helps to know a little history about housing for elders in America.

When I was growing up in the 1930s and 1940s, it was common for different generations of families to live together in the same household. Most aging people lived with their families, who took care of them at home until their death. (Where I grew up may have made a big difference; Philadelphia is famous for its row houses, which are tall and usually narrow and share common walls. Many families, especially if they were of the same ethnicity—like Italians—lived in very close proximity, occupying block after block; and it was typical for several generations of the same family to live in each home.) At any rate, housing for elders was not a topic of major discussion back then, at least that I heard about as a child or an adolescent.

Unbeknownst to me, however, large numbers of Americans had been moving out of rural farming areas and into crowded urban cities for work opportunities since the Industrial Revolution. Most elders couldn't work these new strenuous, mechanized jobs, and more family members working full-time also meant that elders could no longer be cared for in increasingly crowded apartments. An enormous tuberculosis epidemic in the early 1900s didn't help.

This growing housing and welfare crisis for low-income elders led the US government to create Social Security in 1935; the US Department of Housing and Urban Development (HUD), Medicare, and Medicaid in 1965; and supportive housing in subsequent decades. But this also attracted private developers, who sensed a lucrative market for more affluent elders.

Today, elder housing ranges from upscale, private-pay assisted-living facilities for residents who are largely healthy and independent, all the way to memory care facilities whose residents require full-time supervision and intensive medical needs. In between is congregate housing, where residents live in their own private apartments but can access shared services such as transportation, meals, housekeeping, planned activities, health monitoring, personal laundry, and outings. And there are rehabilitative facilities that offer patients temporary transitional care after long hospital stays or surgery before returning home.

The first modern assisted-living facility opened in Oregon in 1983, which allowed private rooms with locked doors as well as separate areas for social interaction. Many variations have followed since. Some accommodate single residents or offer larger double apartments for couples; others offer weekly recreation, transportation, entertainment, and extensive nursing services as the need arises. The larger communities are quite costly with various payment methods—sometimes a sizable purchase price akin to a mortgage, with rebates upon the resident's demise. Very few of these places are available to low-income residents or those on government assistance.

Successful elderly housing can be effective if properly designed, but I have found most of these places limiting. Many times, I've visited these facilities when I was volunteering or trying to locate a senior relative. Their atmosphere is almost always uniformly and starkly depressing: Large community rooms packed full of feeble men and women seated or slumped in chairs and wheelchairs around a

room, many of them dozing or gazing with mostly blank stares at televisions. The residents seem half-asleep and sometimes medicated, with little incentive to be more active. These are not necessarily ill people. But the structure and atmosphere of many of these housing units are very institutional, almost prisonlike, and they certainly cannot truly be called "homes." They seem built more for caregivers rather than the residents themselves. I've always felt depressed after leaving these places and deeply frustrated by what I've seen.

Periodically there have been widely publicized incidents of elder abuse and neglect in some of these places, especially nursing homes and memory care facilities. Despite the enormous responsibility and physical demands, caregiving for the elderly does not pay well. It's difficult to recruit and retain skilled, caring workers, and staff turnover and disruption are frequently high. While some nursing homes offer lovely, attractive environments with humane, professional care and an appealing array of services, others are dismal. They also tend to segregate the elderly from other age groups, which adds to a sense of exclusion and isolation. There is perhaps a growing realization of the limits of the original senior housing or nursing home concept, and in recent years, signs are pointing to change.

Maggie Kuhn and Intergenerational Housing

I first discovered Maggie Kuhn in the late 1980s when I became interested in the concept of intergenerational housing, in which both elders and young people live in the same residence. Why is this important? It embodies many of my goals for inclusion, efficiency, and community with its advantages of economy and the opportunity for both groups to learn from each other, share wisdom, and discover new experiences and perspectives.

A charismatic activist and determined feminist with innovative, creative ideas on racial and gender equity, shared housing, and eldercare, Kuhn inspired me with her deep activism, courage, and passion. "Keep out of the way" was her style—being passive and playing bingo and shuffleboard were not for her.

Outraged at being forced by her employer into the then-mandatory retirement at the age of sixty-five, she founded the Gray Panthers in 1970, an organization that facilitates intergenerational collaboration and social justice against age discrimination. Kuhn became an outspoken national figure, appearing on *The Tonight Show*, *The Phil Donahue Show*, and *The Today Show* several times.

In 1988, I went to visit her three-story home on Greene Street in the Germantown section of Philadelphia to find out more about the National Shared Housing Resource Center (NSHRC), which she founded in 1980. Here, I observed young women in their thirties in the kitchen mingling, talking, and eating with older women in a warm, friendly atmosphere. This large house provided sleeping accommodations for up to six or seven residents at the time.

Maggie Kuhn, pioneer of anti-ageism movement and intergenerational housing.

Kuhn believed that seniors and young people living in the same shared home would benefit both generations, and she started NSHRC to increase the availability of shared housing programs throughout the United States. At one time, this nonprofit organization had more than four hundred programs across America; it now works closely with Homeshare International, which lists homeshare resources in seventeen different countries.

Unfortunately, I was not able to meet Kuhn on my visit. But, as a real estate developer, I did leave deeply inspired to find a site where I could carry out my vision of this type of practical housing. Soon I developed a plan for such a place in a section of Philadelphia called *Manayunk*. This older, working-class neighborhood in the lower northwest section of the city had been gentrified in the 1970s and was named a national historic district in 1982. I located a large scenic lot partially owned by the city behind Main Street, facing the Schuylkill River.

To be an ideal site for intergenerational housing, I felt that a place must have three requirements: (1) Be close to public transportation; (2) be within easy walking access to stores, galleries, and restaurants; and (3) be accessible to schools, banks, and a post office. My concept for this project was a low-rise, two-story building for younger single people, families with small children, and single-parent families, joined by a taller, quieter, elevator-equipped, five-story building for elders on the other side of the lot. The property would also feature a courtyard, gardens, picnic tables, a playground, and even a swimming pool (feasible because the lot came with a city-owned pool that was not being used).

How beneficial it would be for the working parent to know that their young child could come home from school and have an elder (a grandparent or an "adopted" one) there to meet them—no need to hire extra childcare! I envisaged that a child might enjoy creating a new wooden toy or cultivating a garden with an elder person; or perhaps elders could teach cooking, baking, woodworking, or sewing classes after school, among other skills. Opportunities would abound for residents of both buildings to mix and mingle, with a wide variety of community socials, parties, holiday events, barbecues, garage sales, and other activities.

Equipped with preliminary sketches and plans, I presented them to the mayor of Philadelphia and began negotiations to purchase the site. The city was excited and receptive, but then I ran into a major obstacle. The remaining portion of the property not owned by the city was tied up in a custody battle with the heirs of the property. As hard as my attorney, the realtor, and I tried to negotiate, I was unable to purchase this land, and thus I had to give up this dream for intergenerational housing in Manayunk. It was another hard lesson that plans do not always turn out, no matter what the ultimate worth would be to the city, the community, and its residents.

I tried again in 1979, when I approached the township of Absecon to propose an elder housing project in their community. Being a developer of a major real estate project in a municipality, no matter what its size, necessitates an ungodly amount of negotiation, financing, and even legislation among many, many stake-holders. Unfortunately, mortgage rates at that time were rising, and we could not obtain the necessary financing.

I felt disappointed then and still do now!

The Present and Future of Intergenerational Housing

The landscape of growing older in America is thankfully changing, due to the burgeoning baby boomer population. By 2030, all Baby Boomers will be older than sixty-five, and one in five Americans will be at retirement age. These folks are not content to placidly lounge in rocking chairs for the rest of their golden years; they

Bridge Meadows is an intergenerational housing community in Portland, Oregon, that provides affordable housing and other support to adoptive families and elders. A new initiative in Reno, Nevada, will pair young women aging out of foster care with senior citizens eligible for affordable housing.

want to retire later, stay active, have fun, and engage in the same activities and energy that younger people are enjoying.

Generations United is a nonprofit based in Washington DC that improves the lives of children, youth, and older adults by promoting intergenerational collaboration, programs, and policies. According to GU's website, two out of three Americans would like to spend time with those outside their age group, and 92 percent of Americans believe that intergenerational activities can help reduce loneliness.

This last fact is especially important: Loneliness is a central problem in our lives, and more people of every age are keenly aware of it because of our recent unprecedented COVID-19 pandemic. Staying connected with family and yet physically isolated for health reasons became extraordinarily difficult.

Our modern lifestyles are also contributing profoundly to our loneliness. It often seems we'd rather be preoccupied with our electronic devices than talking face to face in person. People are busy and working too much in fast-paced lifestyles. We may think we're more connected than ever via 24/7 text messaging and social media, but in reality, isolation and alienation lurk everywhere, seriously degrading our life, health, and attention spans. This is a time for all ages to rethink their priorities and relationships—and signs are brewing that they are.

The benefits of intergenerational communities cannot be underestimated. The increased social capital between age groups is obvious, for such communities offer opportunities to make new friends and relationships, learn different skills, and cultivate bonds that are more personal, intimate, and deeper as opposed to the more businesslike and somewhat detached ones with institutional caregivers. Intergenerational housing also gives older people a purpose and a way to impart their life wisdom, skills, and experience, which holds real implications for health and longevity. It can also help ease economic burdens on working parents who must otherwise pay (or pay more) for childcare.

In fact, "grandfamilies" is a relatively new term, even if a certain percentage of grandparents have historically always reared grandchildren. According to Generations United as of 2021, nearly eight million children live in households headed by grandparents or other older relatives and at least nineteen grandfamily housing programs exist with onsite services across the United States, financed by a mix of public and private funding. It's encouraging that developers are finally starting to pay attention to this segment with examples such as Bridge Meadows in Portland, Oregon, and Pemberton Park for GrandFamilies in Kansas City, Missouri. Maggie Kuhn's vision is resurging and gaining traction.

AGING AND COURAGE

What does courage mean when it comes to aging?

One of the very real and terrifying parts of aging is the prospect of losing our physical health, mental ability, and independence. For many of us, being independent means not having to ask for anything—and not wanting something that we couldn't get for ourselves. Dependence on others is something most of us deeply dread and resist partly because we hate feeling vulnerable, and we mistakenly equate vulnerability with weakness. It's important to talk about dependence honestly and not think of it as a character flaw.

I myself have had to consider these questions: *How can I still be in control if I cannot think clearly? If I cannot walk? When I must ask someone to drive me to the doctor's office or the supermarket? What exactly am I in control of?* We must understand that life as we are given it offers many benefits, some of which we accept and others we ignore. All of us have tribulations, some of which we overcome and others we carry deep inside, unable or unwilling to shed.

You can remember this: *I'm in control of being grateful for the time I've been fortunate to spend on this earth. I'm in control of offering my thanks to my children for the joy and pride they have given me. I'm in control of being a pleasant, smiling person. And I'm in control of my presence and how I can receive the people who are here to help me. I can appreciate them and let them know that I do. I'm also not too proud to ask for help (although it doesn't come easily). And I'm grateful for that help because I know I need it, and that fact does not diminish me.*

It's important to address courage around aging honestly and openly because it's rarely talked about. Aging people usually are not comfortable acknowledging their fear of declining and dying. People can be afraid to make life choices that might make them happier, such as getting a divorce. Losing a beloved spouse to illness is especially difficult. Both men and women fear being alone or that they might not find another partner.

We need courage. The courage to face the years ahead. The years without spouses as providers and companions, the years alone in bed, the years of declining health, and the years potentially without adequate funding, safety, medical care, and general well-being. To have courage, one must admit and confront fear and reality—then do something constructive about it, preferably earlier than later. We tend to underestimate the resources needed for shelter, food, medical care, and other necessities as we age.

What does one do in these circumstances? Go without a need? Refuse to have coffee with a friend, a family member, or a grandchild out of shame and lack of money? Do we face the issue, or believe things "just happen" and that we'll be taken care of somehow? No, they don't just happen—we need to act. What should we do?

Get a loan from a friend or relative? Usually not. We're too proud to admit that there is even a need. Find a part-time job? Come now—at the age of seventy-two, who will hire me? After all, I hear the media say that firms are not hiring seniors, especially senior women. Is that really true?

Let's take an inventory. What skills do I have? What gifts do I have? How is my physical strength? Mental acuity? What are my assets? Have I really thought about my assets at seventy-two? Or seventy-nine or eighty-eight? Forget that number and get that courage going!

To put it another way: Have the courage to look at yourself in the mirror and accept that you've gotten older. You may not be happy about it, especially if you think that you were once very attractive when you were younger. *Hmm, I'm not really excited about how things have changed, but I can take better care of myself and get more rest and exercise. Get more involved. Don't give up.*

Yes, you're entering another stage of life, but learn to accept who you are now. Learn courage. Acknowledge, not avoid!

I was inspired to write about this because I'm tired of hearing older people, especially women, lamenting pejoratively, declaring "I'm not what I used to be; I can't do all the things I used to do, and it is what it is. I'm physically not able, and I just have to accept getting older." In my opinion, they're not looking at the situation's many benefits: fewer obligations, more financial security (hopefully), and more leisure time to pursue a different career, hobbies, or volunteering opportunities that they always wanted to try. Most of all, they can probably now take the time to be grateful for the age they are.

WHAT WE CAN DO TO STOP BEING AGEIST

Now that we know more about ageism, what do we do about it and how can we avoid perpetuating it? (And keep in mind that many of these principles apply to all age groups.)

If you're an elder:

- Speak up. Don't let yourself be pushed around by others just because you're older.

- Engage in the world and stay curious about it as much as you can. People who stay active mentally are healthier and happier.

- Be positive. It not only makes you feel better but other people too.

- Stay as independent as you can for as long as possible.

- Stay as active and involved for as long as you can.

- Surround yourself with younger people. Their outlook and energy are contagious.

- Take an inventory of your skills, work, habits, hobbies, and family relationships. Think about what they mean to you and how you can cultivate them to create the garden you want.

- Civility applies to all ages. It is incumbent on elders to not take offense, be defensive, or act annoyed if someone offers to help out of kindness and consideration.

- Remember that how you see yourself is often how others will treat you. Ageism is contagious and self-perpetuating.

If you're a younger person:

- Be more conscious of being considerate to everyone. Cultivate politeness, common respect, and an awareness of each person individually and not as a group.

- Pay attention to how ageism is perpetuated in the little things, like what you say and the labels, thoughts, and stereotypes that might automatically come to mind.

- Teach your children by example how to respect and value elders.

- Never assume you know what any person is like until you have spent quality time with them. Making instant judgments is a natural, automatic human trait; acting upon them without thinking is where you run into trouble.

- If you see an elder struggling, ask politely to offer help; don't assume that they are helpless. There's a fine balance between helping and overstepping.

And don't be offended if they reject your offer or are cranky about it. They may just be having a bad day or not feeling well, and their attitude has nothing to do with you personally.

- Don't be afraid to talk to people of age groups different from you. Elders can especially surprise and delight with their wisdom, experience, and life stories.

- Stay aware of what's going on around you and don't be so engrossed in yourself or in your devices. The essence of relationships is how to *be with people, face to face*. That's a skill we're losing. Truly be with real people and not just through email, social media, and text messaging.

- Remember that how you see yourself is often how others will treat you. Just like the flu, ageism is contagious.

11
SPECIAL PEOPLE AND INFLUENCES

Uncle Emil ~ Marsha ~ Natalie ~ Ayn Rand ~
Abraham Lincoln ~ Carl Jung ~
Leonardo da Vinci ~ Maggie Kuhn

Through closeness with others, I came to appreciate kindness.
— Florence Klein —

Of all the means which wisdom acquires to ensure happiness
throughout the whole of life, by far the most important is friendship.
— Epicurus —

I have always appreciated the special people in my life, whether they were relatives, friends, or people I admire. They provided love, wisdom, direction, and companionship. We shared mutual trust, confidentiality, and steadiness that could be counted on in times of difficulty.

What do I desire most in a friend? What attracts me to them? Values, honesty, intelligence, knowledge. A person who listens sincerely, not distractedly. Someone who is dependable whether it's an emergency or I just had an uncomfortable day. Someone I can talk to without judgment and who is willing to be a sounding board.

I also love having different friends for different reasons and at different times. Friendship is like concentric circles: There are moments when one's friendship stands on different lines of the circle. Sometimes it is closer to the center of the circle; at other times a friend may move two lines away but come back later. The key thing is not to get upset if they move around or away—you and they may just be in different places, both literally and psychically. It doesn't have to mean that anything is damaged or changed.

True friends make you feel comfortable and cared about when they're concerned about you. Or when they listen, or when they provide support without lecturing, or when they're always offering advice. And especially when they're fun (which is far more important to me now than back when I was younger).

How do you find good friends, or know when a person might become a worthy one? Think about whom you want to be around or emulate. Who is even worth your time to associate with? It's been said that we are the company we keep. Stay away from people who are toxic.

Don't be afraid to actively cultivate a friendship with someone who is not just like you when it comes to social class, economic status, background, and even political and ideological views. There is always plenty to learn from each other if we both remain open to listening, being respectful, sharing ideas and perspectives, and finding what's common between us rather than conflicting.

Be aware that relationships can change over time. What is most important to me is steadiness and discretion, but we're all different in what we seek and need when it comes to desires, receptivity, and boundaries. Authenticity and genuineness are important, especially in this day and age of social media and instant Facebook "friends." Don't rush to judge.

And be selective. It's always better to cultivate a few true friends than many superficial ones. Quality over quantity!

Uncle Emil
Intelligence, Humor, and Free Spirit

My Uncle Emil, who was my mother's little brother, was not just my dearest relative, but also the best uncle a little girl could have. I was his smiling niece, and he was a true friend and supporter from the very beginning. I was about six and a half when I was visiting his mother, my beloved Grandma Ida, and he took me to see my very first movie, *Gone with the Wind*, at the Greenwood Theater in Trenton, New Jersey.

When I was in his presence, I always felt his warmth, his love, and his sparkling brown eyes. He would hold my hand as we crossed the street, not just out of safety but also because he was an affectionate person. This simple act was very precious and special to me because I did not receive much physical affection from my mother or Grandma Ida. The shimmering joy I felt in just being with him, whether we were walking in a park or he was showing me the best running form, never left me.

Emil saw something special in me from the time I was very young. He was perhaps the person who influenced me the most, always encouraging me in everything I tried—no matter how unusual it might seem to my mother or anyone else. His belief in me and positivity are why my bond with him increased every year until his death in 1983. I loved his honesty, and rarely did I ever turn to anyone else for advice while he was alive. I had a relationship with him that I lacked with both of my husbands in terms of support and openness.

My beloved uncle Emil, a man full of life, running in a marathon in San Francisco.

Emil was fourteen years younger than my mother, Ruth. They were unusually close; she had taken care of him from his birth, including bathing him until he was a teenager. Emil and Ruth's father was rarely around. As often as I visited Grandma Ida—during all the school holidays and in the summer—I never once met my grandfather. Cousin Anna and I believe that my mother's psychosis may have partly stemmed from the absence of her father and her perverse relationship with her brother, but we'll never really know. Eventually, Emil broke free of his overprotective, anxious sister and the emotional stoniness of his mother—certainly, his expansive personality was the total opposite of theirs.

Emil was quick-witted, sharp, and funny. "Exuberant" was the word to describe him. Not surprisingly, he had a great sense of humor, always armed with a new joke he was eager to tell and ready to laugh with a loud guffaw. In his teenage years, he'd hop on empty freight train cars just to see what the world was like on the other side of his hometown of Trenton. He also wanted to be an actor, but he needed to work instead. Then came World War II and he was drafted in 1942, putting an end to his acting dreams.

Emil's true love was a woman named Arista. She was from a Greek family in New Jersey, and they got married and had two children together. Since Arista was not Jewish, Ida did not acknowledge her. Later, Emil and Arista moved to Riverside, California, where they established a business called Economy Window Cleaners. This was a far cry from Emil's acting ambitions in the theater, but he had to earn a living for his family. Sadly, Arista died when Phyliss was around seven and Lewis five. About a year later, Emil met Bernice, a music teacher in the local school, and they got married.

Emil was a most unusual man, a maverick in many ways. Highly intelligent, he was extremely well-read with an amazing memory. I traveled to California every year to see him, and we'd walk, share stories and insights, talk, do more walking, and talk some more. One year, as we started down a hiking trail, I recall asking him a single question: *Emil, what is the history of religion?* With no notes or hesitation, he started telling me the history of religion, just like that. (Not that he himself was religious, mind you, but he knew enough about the subject that he could fluently discuss the basis for it. His depth of knowledge and understanding of the world were unbelievable.)

He was also very athletic, physical, and sensual. He loved running, and sometimes he'd sprint half-naked across an Oakland park near his house whenever he got a chance or wasn't being chased by a guard. He once ran a marathon across the Golden Gate Bridge. He adored dancing and would go to community dances every month around Oakland and San Francisco. In fact, he met his third wife, Juliana, at a dance and they got married when he was seventy.

I remember one evening when Emil was visiting me and my family when I was living in Dresher, Pennsylvania. He asked if there was any place nearby where we could go dance. I was in my fifties then and couldn't think of any such place, as that was really not my scene. But I did recall that there was usually a wedding happening on Saturday nights at a rental hall not too far from my home. Before I knew it, my sister-in-law Sharon and I put on appropriate attire and makeup, the three of us got into the car, and we arrived at a large wedding reception unannounced. Emil, Sharon, and I crashed the party just after the formal ceremony. A large band was playing, sounding good. We just blended in with the numerous invited guests—either side of the family must have thought we were related to the other. We stayed, danced for an hour, had great fun, and left.

Emil cared little about money or travel, but he was a loyal friend to all kinds of people. He always knew what was happening in the country, the world, and the larger universe. But he hated politicians. He subscribed to so many magazines that they'd accumulate every week; the piles would grow high next to his sofa until Juliana cleared them out.

He also wrote poems. This one was from May 1967:

> *Black brother,*
> *Black brother*
> *Forgive me*
>
> *My skin is white.*
> *Your hates and fears*
> *Sear me*
> *Thru and Thru*
>
> *My self-hatred equals yours.*
> *Brother.*
> *I'll wait for you.*
> *When we can meet*
> *And you can love me*
> *As I love you.*

I still have quite a few of his poems. He wrote to me often and was especially proud of me when I began working as a stockbroker and started moving up in my career as an investment professional. In the fall of 1997, he sent me this letter:

> *Dearest Flo:*
>
> *With reference to our conversation of last night, I feel compelled to tell you what you already know: That unless the laws of human nature are repealed, you as a female and as a Jew will garner conscious or unconscious jealousy and opposition at Kidder Peabody in inverse proportion to the degree of your success. It makes no difference how politic*

and diplomatic you are. The higher your rise may be, somewhere, somehow in this lovely organization that you now find yourself in, you will find ungrateful wretches who will, even in the face of their own self-interest, oppose you.

So … please wear heavy gloves and expect thorns whilst dallying amongst the roses. And … have fun.

With love,
Emil

Emil never smoked cigarettes and was an early proponent of yogurt, fruit, and organic foods. But one terrible evening, I received a call from Juliana that Emil was in the hospital. He had had a stroke at the age of seventy-three. I flew out to see him and stayed a few days. He was able to come home in a week or so, but his speech was severely impaired. This was a terrible blow for Emil and the rest of us.

He underwent a very long rehabilitation, during which he saw many doctors, and he worked very conscientiously to speak well enough to be understood. It was cruel in a way: He had always wanted to act, but now that he had the time, he couldn't because of his speech impediment. His laughter, always loud and hearty before, would erupt at odd times after his stroke. Finally, after months of arduous work and recovery, he was able to play bridge. Juliana even wrote a book about Emil's stroke and recovery.

We still went walking when I visited him in California during these difficult months. I recall one sunny afternoon when we had a fascinating discussion about the universe—the stars and the planets. I could always understand him, even if his words were slurred.

About three years after the stroke, he was diagnosed with lung cancer, even though he had never smoked. The cancer lingered for another year and so did he. Then my special person was gone, and I have never quite recovered since.

MARSHA
A Good Mind—and a Listener without Judgment
Starting when I was about four, we moved from Philadelphia to Brooklyn and then back to different areas of Philly many times in a short period. As a result, I never developed close friendships and had very few girlfriends during my early years. I often hear stories from others about kindergarten relationships that have lasted through decades of marriage, children, and so on. I have none of those memories. Because of that, I have never taken friendships for granted. So, it was extraordinarily special to begin a friendship with Marsha when we both lived in Center City.

I first met Marsha in 1964 at a children's birthday party that I was attending with friends of Len and me in northeast Philadelphia. I was in my early thirties then. An intellectual with a quick mind, she worked for the publisher J. B. Lippincott & Co. After her husband died and their daughters graduated from college, she moved to Center City around 1970. We became close friends when I moved into the Chocolate Factory in Old City in 1982, just three blocks from her apartment.

I admired Marsha's honesty, straightforwardness, dedication to Jewish traditions, and intelligence. We were very different as women. I was gutsy, a risk-taker, while she was parsimonious and cautious. Me: generous, decisive; Marsha: quiet, deliberate.

We'd talk and chat about what she was doing at work with the Jewish publishing company and what I was doing in the brokerage and real estate industries. I listened to her disagreements with her supervisors and then I'd suggest different ways to look at the situation.

She did not know anything about construction or renovations, but she was an amazing listener nonetheless. I discussed all my issues with her, and she was always attentive and interested. On a day when I might be quite upset with lawyers or the many building and finance issues that would come up (which are quite normal during construction projects), I'd call Marsha.

"Hi, Marsh, will you meet me at the Society Hill Hotel?" I'd ask.

And she always met me. She listened, never judged me, did not give advice, and always supported me! Marsha would quietly say, "Florence, you always manage to come out ahead no matter how difficult the situation may be." She had faith in me.

We regularly went for walks around the historic Society Hill neighborhood, and because we were both curious about the constant renovations going on in many of the row houses we passed, we enjoyed peeking in the windows to see how things were coming along.

I remember that she always wanted a fur coat but never wanted to spend the money on one. It took a bit of convincing on my part until she bought one. She really enjoyed that coat when she walked to work on cold, snowy days. She never wore flashy clothes, but she did love shoes.

I had a car in town and Marsha didn't, so one day I picked her up and we decided to drive to New York City to find good Brooklyn bagels, see a show, and say hello to her daughter Jane. I decided to be adventurous and actually go over the Brooklyn Bridge, and boy, did we get lost! After a number of absurd turns and backtracking, we began to feel famished. But when we stopped to go into a Hasidic store to buy bagels, the men refused to speak to us. It was a very religious Jewish Orthodox neighborhood in which men did not speak directly to women without an introduction by a known man.

It was all a little scary. We had gotten more than a little lost and hungry driving around until I found the Brooklyn Bridge and could return safely to New York City. We laughed many times over the years about trying to find the best bagels in Brooklyn.

NATALIE
A Quality, Caring Person Who Woke Me Up to Myself

I met Natalie in the spring of 2012 when she was advising my daughter Karen in her election campaign to become a Superior Court judge in Kitsap County, Washington. Natalie was extremely involved and knowledgeable in politics and knew all the players, including the Governor. She and I immediately bonded and felt exceptional warmth toward each other.

The very night I met her, she started to tell me the story of her husband. At the time, I was a bit surprised as it was not the usual thing that one says to a stranger in a darkened pub-style restaurant. We became friendly and we'd meet for lunch or at political events on Bainbridge Island or at her favorite restaurant in Silverdale. Natalie shared many of her life's adventures, family joys, and sorrows with me. She had so many friends with whom she was involved over the years, and she was always giving sage advice, helping with gifts, and giving generously to the many organizations. She never forgot a birthday, a thank-you, or a friend's funeral.

Natalie also suffered from many medical problems, but these did not keep her from going to events, dressed up in attractive blue or peach clothes, and looking beautiful. No one would ever guess that she was seriously ill. She never asked me to visit her when she was not feeling well, but I just showed up to help and I know she appreciated my caring.

Natalie was originally from Massachusetts, brought up by loving parents. We often compared the contrast in our backgrounds. Natalie was a fabulous home cook, baker, and hostess, while my mother never had any company over at our home, nor were her meals inspiring. Since Natalie and I were both night owls, we'd speak almost every evening, discussing politics, our values, and our families.

It was through many of these moments that I found out about myself. Natalie would say, "Florence, you have no idea what you look like when you walk into a room. You do not realize the impression you make." I'd listen, wondering what she really meant. But, because I deeply valued and admired her, her words began to sink in and I finally began to understand who I am. Gosh, it sure took me a long time!

Recalling the many, many times we were together over the years from 2012 to 2018, I think of her often. After she died, more than 250 mourners showed up, and I felt honored to have been considered one of her close friends.

AYN RAND
Unwavering Individualist

As a child sneaking into the adult section of the Logan Library to find more exciting books, I discovered *The Fountainhead* by Ayn Rand, published in 1943. At ten or eleven years of age, I had no idea how radical and controversial the ideas presented in that book were. The author's goal was to present the ideal man, with the theme of the individual versus the collective, seated not in politics but in men's souls. She emphasized the importance of being an individual—which was revolutionary at that time. As I look over the quotes of Ayn Rand:

"The question isn't who is going to let me, it's who is going to stop me."

"A creative man is motivated by the desire to achieve, not by the desire to beat others."

"I swear by my life and my love of it that I will never live for the sake of another man, nor ask another man to live for mine."

I now realize how much these ideas have shaped so many of the principles I've lived by most of my life. The hero in *The Fountainhead* was an architect who chose to follow his own new ideas rather than the standard methods. Earlier in this book, I wondered where I got the ideas to be interested in buildings and developing condominiums in Philadelphia. Perhaps many of Ayn Rand's ideas influenced me more than I'd realized.

ABRAHAM LINCOLN
Moral, Flexible, Compassionate Leader

Like many children learning about our country's history, I always admired President Abraham Lincoln. I've been enamored by his goals, his compassion, his ability to be flexible and change directions as ethically and morally needed, and his skill in leading a nation. Even before witnessing the bewildering dysfunction of today's politics, I had always been impressed with Lincoln's ability to work with members of opposite parties—Republicans, Democrats, and his own Whig party—and even his willingness to invite three rivals to his own cabinet: William H. Seward as Secretary of State, Salmon P. Chase as Secretary of the Treasury, and Edward Bates as Attorney General.

His clear vision of himself from an early age acknowledged that he wanted to be President of the United States. As a person who did not quite realize who I was until eighty-two years old, I find this astonishing.

I also read about his empathy for the women who were left behind in the Civil War when their husbands and sons went to fight and many never returned home. One woman wrote a letter to tell him of her misfortunes, and he invited her to come speak with him in his office. How rare a human he was!

CARL JUNG
Innate Individuation

I was not introduced to this important Swiss psychiatrist until I was in my forties. He is well known for his theories of extroversion, introversion, the psychological types that led to the foundation for the Myers-Briggs test, and many more revolutionary ideas. He believed, as I do, that we are born with an innate nature that acts as a blueprint for life, and I can see for myself that the environment that I grew up in during the first twelve years of my life was not the person I grew into. Jung continues to fascinate me. Here is one of my favorite quotes of his: "Everything that irritates us about others can lead us to an understanding of ourselves."

LEONARDO DA VINCI
The Original Renaissance Man

Known for his painting, sculpture, drawing, and his contributions to science, engineering, architecture, and anatomy, this amazing man's diversity, breadth, talent, and depth astound me the more I read and learn about him. To think that, around 1490, during the height of the Renaissance more than five centuries ago, he thought about the possibility of flying machines.

I saw his world-famous painting of the Mona Lisa at the Louvre Museum about ten years ago. Because this woman's face is so familiar from books and the media, I felt surprised by its gentleness once I stood before the actual painting, I would love to go back and see her again. There is so much more to learn about the genius of Leonardo di ser Piero da Vinci.

Maggie Kuhn

An Activist at Heart

As I relate in the Ageism chapter, Maggie Kuhn has profoundly influenced me. In a *New York Times* article on September 8, 2020, author Susan J. Douglas declared that Maggie Kuhn is "all but forgotten." But I have not forgotten her, and I assume others have not forgotten all that this woman accomplished. She was a passionate activist and feminist who founded the Gray Panthers movement in 1970 to combat social injustice, racial and gender inequity, and elder discrimination. She later started the National Shared Housing Resource Center to encourage intergenerational housing.

Kuhn inspired me. I am an activist at heart, and like Maggie, I am interested in many areas that I feel strongly about. And when I see a need, I usually do not wait to be called—instead I move forward to see if I can make a difference.

12
RANDOM THOUGHTS, PLEASURES, AND REFLECTIONS

**On Creativity ~ On Enjoyment ~ How to Navigate Today's World ~
Reading Is Joy ~ Antidotes to Loneliness ~ On Jigsaw Puzzles ~
The Questions I Ask Myself ~ Hiking on Sundays ~
On Stress ~ If I Had to Do It Again ~ Revelations in My Eighth Decade**

*And this I believe that the free exploring mind of the individual human
is the most valuable thing in the world.*
— *Albert Einstein* —

ON CREATIVITY

The velocity of change over my lifetime has been amazing! I have been saying this for many years. At the age of nearly eighty-seven, I read Ken Robinson's book, *Out of Our Minds*. For the first time, I realized why I've always done things differently from others, why I've always been a trailblazer, and why I've never stopped inventing new ideas to improve the systems I decided, God knows why, needed help or change. No one but me made these decisions. Were they always right or successful? No, but they were mine—*creative*: a word I never thought of as describing myself. Now, at this age, I cannot stop.

Looking back, I enjoyed working in the field of finance, advising many types of clients and figuring out satisfactory investment decisions for them. And even though I never considered myself creative, I realize now that seeking out real estate properties, envisioning their potential use, and completing their transformation also truly touched the creative side of Florence.

ON ENJOYMENT

I feel so blessed in my life that I have enjoyed and experienced so much and there is still so much to look forward to. I do not tend to look back on what I could have accomplished or experienced.

How to Navigate Today's World

1. Find out early who you are.
2. Listen to your inner voice.
3. Be humble, but do not denigrate yourself.
4. Do not be influenced by changing trends.
5. Find one or two close friends … ones whom you truly admire. They may not be just like you, but they do need to have the same values.
6. Find a mentor in your work.
7. Find a love who thinks you are special. Acknowledge them.
8. Be kind to yourself.
9. Do not let your life slip through your fingers by living in the past or for the future.
10. By living your life one day at a time, you live all the days of your life.

Reading Is Joy

Since I was a small child, I have always cherished books. I used to hide a flashlight under the covers while hungrily devouring the adventures of Nancy Drew and Mary Poppins. Today, I read mostly nonfiction, biographies, history, or philosophy. The Sunday version of the *New York Times* (print version only) is still the simplest treat, along with a bagel with lox, onion, and tomato, accompanied by a cup of good coffee. My favorite activity is to find a quiet stream, lean against a stout tree, and read! It isn't surprising that there are still books on my shelves that I haven't read.

Antidotes to Loneliness

- Find a new friend.
- Just talk to someone at the grocery checkout line.
- Get a pet.
- Share a home with an old friend.
- Playing Scrabble with friends is fun. It's even better with English teachers!
- Join a social club.

On Jigsaw Puzzles

I have always loved them! The harder and more challenging they are, the better. I always finish them—even if it sometimes takes months. I have especially close friends with whom I have vacationed on various holidays, and we usually work on puzzles together. Come to think of it, two new puzzles are waiting for me now.

THE QUESTIONS I ASK MYSELF

You might think, from reading this memoir and with all that I accomplished in my career, that I was always sure of what I was doing. But however successful or "put-together" I seemed, there were times of doubt and challenge.

In late 2022, I was finishing the book and preparing to move to a new apartment. In sorting through my stuff, I came across a diary I had forgotten about in which I'd jotted down a hundred questions in 2010. It was fascinating to read the thoughts I'd written on its pages and what was on my mind then. Many are still just as relevant today.

- How can I make my time more meaningful?
- How can I enrich my children's lives?
- When can I take the *time* to think?
- How can I simplify my life?
- What mistakes do I regret?
- Are women afraid of me?
- Where are the old friends?
- Why have I not kept my old friends?
- How can I turn Silver Planet into a more successful company?
- What are my true talents?
- Why is it difficult to find friends in Colorado?
- Am I really a snob?
- What are my fears?
- What are my ambitions?
- How can I be more involved in helping women?
- Why do I need only six hours of sleep?
- Why don't I cook much?
- What does *not* going to yoga and Pilates mean?
- Shall I abandon Silver Planet?
- Why continue to wear hats?
- Where can I go next?
- When can I retain more of the knowledge I read?
- Why do I hang on too long? Men, clothes, etc.
- When can I stop, smell the roses, and live in the moment?
- Is my honesty a virtue with others?
- Should I change my hair color? Why?
- Can I take a six-month sabbatical?
- Who do I admire the most?
- Why can't I sort the jewelry drawers?

- Why do I appear so far out and different to so many people?
- Why does Africa draw me?
- What makes me feel good in a day?
- Do I avoid intimacy?
- What is important?
- Who is important?
- How can I be more responsive?
- When can I go back to Italy?
- What else can I do to make a difference?

HIKING ON SUNDAYS

After my divorce from Len, I joined an intrepid hiking group. It was a great way to get exercise, meet new people, and test my endurance. Exploring previously unknown parks and rappelling down slopes sure was a welcome change from watching the ticker tape of the stock market.

ON STRESS

Stress is something you're creating yourself to be miserable about; it's not a physical thing that presides over you, but a construct that people create.

IF I HAD TO DO IT AGAIN

Many times, people have asked me, *What would you have done differently in your life?*

I would not have been such a workaholic. I would have scheduled time to enjoy the physical world of trees and trails, of water and mountains. I spent so many of my days immersed in the responsibility that I felt for my children and careers in finance, building condos, and contributing to organizations. This constituted the desk world to which I tied myself down six or seven days a week. No one insisted that I do this; all my endeavors were self-motivated.

Now, looking back, I would have put on my weekly calendar a time to do yoga, learn to sail a boat, or even just have fun! I would not have majored in business but instead enrolled in university classes in history, psychology, behavior modification, and other similar courses. I would have learned to specialize and do more research in one area, perhaps racism. Now that I'm rediscovering myself, I find that I have a gift of communication, of sensitivity, that can help people.

I would take my time in my twenties to grow as a person. I was married at the age of twenty—way too early. I would have explored Greenwich Village in New York City and tried developing my acting skills. I would have lived in a freer, less structured day that wasn't nine to five. I would have just *hung out*! I never hung out, even to cut school. I never thought of myself as a goody-two-shoes, but maybe I was.

If I had to change careers, I would have gone into psychiatry. I was interested in the mind and how it works. Still am.

I would have allowed passion to well up from the deep recesses in my heart, to feel the oneness with another's body, to be more sensual. To feel the joy of falling in love.

REVELATIONS IN MY EIGHTH DECADE

A friend of mine who has known me for many years recently said to me, "Florence, you scared us," because I was so self-confident in my ventures. This may sound hard to believe, but I was totally unaware of others' perception of me. Frankly, I wish I'd known about myself a lot earlier than in my eighties. It still surprises me to this day. I was just so excited about life, about exploring and discovering new experiences, new countries, and new challenges that I just kept going.

It never occurred to me to seek a mentor. In business or anything else. It just didn't occur to me to have a mentor or ask anybody anything. I wish I would have had one. But then again, since I didn't talk to anyone about myself, others didn't engage back.

Life is so special. I *must* keep moving myself to renew my energy, passion, and desire to do what has inspired and driven me to be who I now know I am. There is still more to me, Florence Klein, and what I can leave to my children, friends, and others.

BOOK DISCUSSION
GROUP QUESTIONS

FAMILY

1. What are the most important values that you can instill in your children?

2. If you want to have a career, would you consider staying home for a time to raise a family?

COURAGE

1. What are you afraid of?

2. What is your risk tolerance? In what area (financial, having a child, changing a career)?

VOLUNTEERING

1. Would you volunteer? If so, where?

2. Would you consider volunteering at an unusual place, like a prison?

AGEISM

1. How does aging affect you? What does the word "old" mean to you?

2. How do you view intergenerational housing? Would you live in one?

3. How do we overcome generational divides?

4. Have you ever experienced age discrimination? (Regardless of whether you're under thirty years of age or more than fifty.)

SPECIAL PEOPLE AND INFLUENCES

1. What people have influenced you the most in your life? And why?

2. What attracts you to certain people or influences?

3. What do you consider the most important qualities of a true friend?

ACKNOWLEDGMENTS

To Mi Ae Lipe: I could not have made this journey without the competence of Mi Ae. Her knowledge, editing, and writing made this memoir all come together. The experience and caring that she provided me, I am forever thankful.

To Jennifer Wilhoit, who probed and poked into the lengthy years of my life with diligence and persistence. Her skill and caring opened my long-forgotten memories.

And to my close friend, Ann Martin, who continued to encourage me to finish this book.

PERMISSIONS AND CREDITS

I gratefully acknowledge all those who granted permission to reprint their material in this book. Every effort has been made to properly credit, trace, and contact copyright holders; if any error or omission has been made, please contact me, and I will be glad to remedy it in future printings of this book.

Chapter 1 | A Philadelphia Childhood

- Pages 2, 3, 7, 9, 11, 16, 17, and 18: Courtesy of Florence Klein and family.

- Page 4: *Row Houses in North Philadelphia*, Dick Swanson, US Environmental Protection Agency, public domain, Wikimedia; Google Street View, Google Maps.

- Page 7: *1942 Schools at War Poster*, Irving Isador Nurick, US Office of Education, public domain, Wikimedia.

Chapter 2 | Adolescent Fun

- Pages 20, 21, 23, 25, and 28: Courtesy of Florence Klein and family.

- Page 22: *Atlantic City Boardwalk Crowd in Front of the Blenheim Hotel in 1911*, Library of Congress, public domain, Wikimedia.

- Page 23: Postcard depicting the Boardwalk and Hotel Traymore, Atlantic City, New Jersey, circa 1916, public domain, Wikimedia.

- Page 24: *Contestants Line Up in Swimsuits at the Miss America Pageant, September 7th to 12th, 1953, Convention Hall, Atlantic City, New Jersey*, Library of Congress, public domain, Wikimedia.

- Page 26: *Remington Rand Bookkeeping Machine, 1944–1950*, David Thompson, Museums Victoria, licensed under CC BY 4.0.

Chapter 3 | A Family of My Own

- Pages 31, 32, 33, 34, 36, 38, 39, 40, 41, 42, 44, 45, 46, 47, and 48: Courtesy of Florence Klein and family.

- Page 35: Courtesy of the Klein family.

Chapter 4 | Trailblazing Stockbroker

- Page 52: Former Robinson & Co. building, original source unknown.

- Page 60: *Philadelphia* magazine, April 1977.

- Pages 62, 65, and 70: Courtesy of Florence Klein and family.

- Page 67: *Union League of Philadelphia*, April 6, 2017, Erik Lattwein, Alamy Stock Photos.

CHAPTER 5 | COURAGE

- Page 75: *Small Woman Carries the Key to Open the Lock*, fcscafeine, iStock.

CHAPTER 6 | REBUILDING HISTORY

- Page 80: Google Maps.

- Page 81: *June 11, 2013: People Visit Elfreth's Alley in Philadelphia*, tupungato, iStock.

- Page 83: *The Hoop Skirt Factory, 309–313 Arch Street*, April 19, 2013, Beyond My Ken, Wikimedia, licensed under CC BY 4.0.

- Page 86: Marquetand's Candy advertisement, public domain, *Philly & Stuff* blog, M. McShea.

- Page 87: *The Bulletin*, June 19, 1981.

- Pages 88, 89, 91, 97, 98, and 100: Courtesy of Florence Klein and family.

- Page 90: Florence and Len Klein in their living room, Tom Crane, *Inside* magazine, Winter 1985, Philadelphia Jewish Exponent.

- Page 94: *South St. Star*, December 4, 1986.

- Pages 93–94 (text): "Dozens of Coffins, Bodies Discovered at Construction Site in Old City," Anita Oh and David Spunt, CBS News Philadelphia, March 9, 2017, https://www.cbsnews.com/philadelphia/news/coffins-discovered-at-construction-site-in-old-city/.

- Page 99 (photo): "Our Historic Rehabbers Get Creative," John Costello, *The Philadelphia Inquirer*, March 9, 1986. From *The Philadelphia Inquirer*, © 1986, Philadelphia Inquirer, LLC, all rights reserved. Used under license.

- Page 101 (text): "Our Historic Rehabbers Get Creative," Gene Austin, *The Philadelphia Inquirer*, March 9, 1986. From *The Philadelphia Inquirer*, © 1986, Philadelphia Inquirer, LLC, all rights reserved. Used under license.

CHAPTER 7 | VOLUNTEERING

- Page 106: *Anne Frank House*, Matthew Sayers, iStock.

- Page 109: Courtesy of Florence Klein and Hadassah (the Women's Zionist Organization of America).

- Page 113: *ADX Cell Design*, January 26, 2015, RicHard-59, Wikimedia, licensed under CC BY-SA 3.0.

CHAPTER 8 | SILVER PLANET

- Page 119: "Local Woman Starts Site for Senior Citizens," Carol McGraw, *Colorado Springs Gazette*, January 30, 2009, https://gazette.com/news/local-woman-starts-site-for-senior-citizens/article_2d8abc6a-3549-559e-9a3b-062500bdedb5.html.

Chapter 9 | Life Changes

- Pages 123, 125, 126, and 127: Courtesy of Florence Klein and family.

Chapter 10 | Ageism

- Page 132: *Multiracial Senior and Young Business People Working inside Modern Office*, Vanessa Nunes, iStock.

- Page 135: *An Elderly Woman Feeling Isolated, Alone, and Cold at Her Home during the Winter Months*, Neil Bussey, iStock.

- Page 136: Courtesy of The Gray Panthers.

- Page 138: Courtesy of Bridge Meadows.

- Page 142: *Young Man and His Senior Father in Wheelchair on a Walk in Town*, Halfpoint, iStock.

Chapter 11 | Special People and Influences

- Page 146: Courtesy of Florence Klein and family.

- Page 152: *Ayn Rand (1943 Talbot Portrait)*, Bobbs-Merrill Company, public domain, Wikimedia; *Abraham Lincoln*, Alexander Gardner and Moses Parker Rice, November 8, 1863, public domain, Wikimedia.

- Page 153: *Jung, Carl Gustav (1875–1961)*, photographer unknown, ETH-Bibliothek, public domain, Wikimedia; *Portrait of Leonardo da Vinci (from Characaturas by Leonardo da Vinci, from Drawings by Wincelslaus Hollar, out of the Portland Museum)*, Leonardo da Vinci, 1786, donated by the Metropolitan Museum of Art, Wikimedia.

Chapter 12 | Random Thoughts, Pleasures, and Reflections

- Page 159: Courtesy of Florence Klein.

CPSIA information can be obtained
at www.ICGtesting.com
Printed in the USA
JSHW042333050723
44051JS00003B/11